Continued Building

Albert Kirchengast

Continued Building on the Village, the Settlement, the City

A Plea

Birkhäuser
Basel

"Isn't everything like it never was?" Botho Strauß

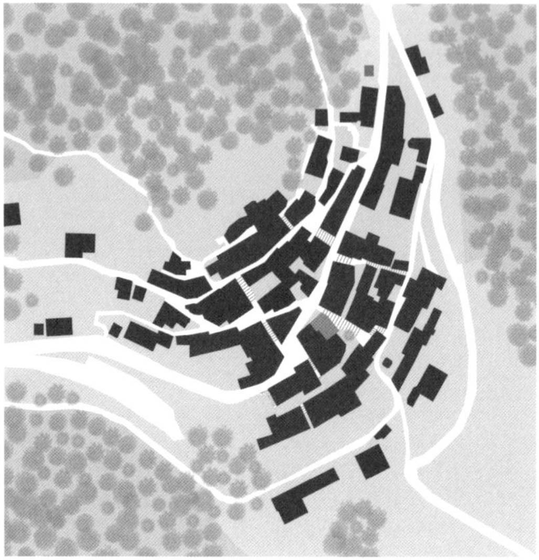

Monte, Val di Muggio/Ticino, location plan with house
Renovation Jonathan Sergison

Resistance

The short text entitled "Resistance" accompanies a monograph that was published in 2002, when the work of Jonathan Sergison and Stephen Bates already enjoyed international attention. The manifesto of the two architects is found at the end of the magazine, illustrated by just two images: of Joseph Beuys's legendary felt suit and of an anonymous brick wall set in an English landscape. The latter image appears so dusky on the paper that the mood is strangely enchanting – as if night is already falling. The grayish tone and the rawness evoke the aura of the timelessly old, unplastered wall, built of gently weathered stones laid in simple courses. We peer, with the two architects, into a corner, where the wall with its beautiful coping changes direction. Our thoughts drift to this place; we feel as if we have been transported to an archaic quadrangle. Animated, towering broad-leafed trees surround the enclosing wall, which restrains the greenery by setting a boundary. The walled space is dominated by a tidily mowed lawn. This is a primeval scene, a *hortus conclusus*, a concrete symbol, and an archaic spatial element, the limitation of the human domain through the act of joining together small bricks to form a wall. Somewhere in the distance, out of shot, stands the house.

The eponymous Resistance, which is so important to the pair and underlies the close relationship between their architecture, anonymous building, and art, is inherent in this setting. It is filled with curious energy – generated by this focus on the elementary materiality of a wall. And it is, of course, more than this: "Architecture is often both object and subject but it may also embody continuity and a re-affirmation of place. It may recognise the imperfection in daily phenomena."[1] This observation of the incidental, of the initially unassuming, and this readiness to confront the everyday underlie their approach and their design. If we look for things, they appear to us: "This architecture contributes to an increased atmospheric density of a place and in this there lies an ultimate resistance to the artificial and the virtual."[2] This is a statement on behalf of the analog, the built world: Place, phenomenon, and atmospheric density are the key terms. We could encounter such scenes ourselves in our daily lives, scenes capable of lending a presence to our thoughts and to our intentions. But these situations must be encountered, and then read; for only if they can be read, can they be shared. In other words, we choose to differentiate between the experience of such a wall and our own work – but would we still make this differentiation if we could learn to understand the atmosphere of such places as both specific and general, as part of our architectural sensibility?

And, hence, there is nothing coincidental or banal about this moment. It is fundamental, because we probably approach it in the same mood. It is the starting point for a phenomenological understanding of architecture and design. The special becomes visible in the ordinary. "Reading" is obviously an inadequate word for the necessary level of attentive devotion because there is no certainty

that any words can get us to the point at which we feel a physical connection. In this context, images are neither tricks nor surrogates but, rather, physical reminders, notes about what could happen if we refer to the elementary origins of architecture. It seems far from unimportant whether the things that we design are a reflection of our hands, ears, or eyes, etc. We intuitively understand that the hand-layered baked earth remains associated with the ground, even when it has assumed the form of a brick or a wall. This powerful example clearly concerns the multilayered continuity of a place, with which we develop an uncanny connection because, our awareness heightened, we encounter both the familiar and the alien. A wall, whose concreteness resonates as we stand before it, touch it, feel it. Anyone who cannot summon up this sensibility is missing something. It is a sensation stimulated by the clever choice of a photograph and underlined by words, but all this is really grounded in the concreteness that is conveyed because we feel drawn to it. This is connected with the imaginary qualities that we also expect in such a place, which hint at its known, suspected, unknown, and yet somehow still shared history – as well as the possible future that we create for it. This "forward-looking" perspective is unavoidably associated with the design process. And if this starts with the presence of things and with their inherent tension, then past and future come together in a concrete way in the experience of *now.* We experience the calmness of the existing as a dimension. And naturally, elsewhere, its lack of calmness.

Felt and brick: The concreteness of objects, which they communicate when they achieve a presence that awakens our attention, combined with a materiality that absorbs both the time at which they were made and the period during which they exist, transforms a simple wall into a work of art. Respect is generated by our awareness of the special qualities of such an everyday object; it is its ability to *move* us in certain situations that guarantees that we will show it the appropriate respect. Or, put another way: Empathy unites spirit and body. The approach also embraces audacity, as represented by the felt suit. This is the work of an artist, whose art transforms the general into the specific, and embodies ideas – just like the above wall. The wall and the suit are united by the work on and with existing objects that enables us to understand ourselves. The fact that such an approach is in contradiction with the dominant practice is probably a consequence of the intensified professionalisation of a discipline, whose discourse has become somewhat remote and self-referential. Even if the design studios of certain universities are increasingly seeking to establish a link with the forms of the past or to appreciate "simple" materiality, and even if Continued Building has become a social issue in times of crisis – whether as a method of *reuse* or as a creative impulse – this is still not the same as employing the impact of the here and now as the starting point of the design, as causatively linking the design process with the Continued Building of the material presence in the space. But why is this so important and not just another way of designing?

Let us return to the place, to the concrete object. We learn that this is the kitchen garden of a Georgian country house. A house that is about as old as Jonathan Sergison's own house, of which we will soon speak. The dating is anchored in its history; we see a three-and-a-half-meter-high wall bracing itself against the topography; gaining character from the rising and falling lines. The beauty of this extremely simple structure is derived from the way in which it reveals the flowing landscape, to which it now belongs. This mutual affirmation transforms the wall into a powerful experience and an act of synergy with its setting: "In these ways the landscape has had a decisive impact on the ultimate character of the wall, with the wall making the landscape more visible on the one hand and the material of the wall becoming more potent on the other. It is as if the landscape has set free the true nature of the wall being both flawed and monumental at the same time."[3] We could also say that a place first emerges from this type of poetic interaction with nature – an interaction that we experience, whether it was intended or not. Poetry means: *hervorbringen* (to bring forth). To give space to what is already *there*. Of course others have been reflecting on this for some time. Christian Norberg-Schulz focused on special places as a means of suggesting how we could sharpen our phenomenological understanding of architecture. He speaks famously of the "Genius Loci" – the spirit of a place – as a way of evoking its prevailing quality, which we can then strengthen – or weaken, or perhaps even destroy. His specific focus is pre-industrial landscapes, composite forms that include houses, farmsteads, and cities and are the product of a particular culture. We experience these places as "phenomena." The Norwegian architect uses this term to describe the interplay of architecture with the natural topography, vegetation, and weather conditions, etc. But this is an interplay that *shows itself.* Norberg-Schulz underlines this at a decisive point with the help of a poem, Georg Trakl's "Winterabend."[4] This poem is also about the sharing of an apparently mundane moment; frugality that suddenly turns into the opposite, an existential transformation that becomes real as soon as we experience it through such verse. The poetry of a moment transforms concrete things into architectural space that interacts decisively with the natural realm, into significant details: threshold, laid table, fireplace, snow on the window, darkness ... someone is returning from a journey that has presented its share of challenges or, simply, from a walk, into a warm, brightly-lit home, which is transformed into an experience by the threshold, the door, the light and the warmth, the hunger and the tiredness, the restful sanctuary, the leaving outside of the rough weather, which now gives this place its meaning because there is something against which it can offer protection. The ordinary can turn into the extraordinary. This transformation requires particular attention. The task is to discover where these objects resonate with our disposition – or, in other words: to identify the moments that facilitate the existential everyday experiences that sustain and give meaning and direction to our own lives.

Generations after Norberg-Schulz's book, the two London architects Jonathan Sergison and Stephen Bates appear to be reformulating *genius loci* for today: "Buildings not only reshape the physical environment and therefore our view of spatial relationships, they also instil an emotive response, based upon association and memory. In this way building is communicative. If acted upon consciously, within a conceptual framework, architecture may go beyond programme and site by engaging with personal and collective experience of place and our position in the world."[5] Building a place means caring for it and giving it time to find itself. The quote is taken from a key text written by the pair that addresses the subject of *tolerance*. They also attach great importance to the precise use of words, as if these embody valuable experience. They speak of "place," rather than of "site" or "program." But their decisive contribution is their understanding of tolerance as an ambivalent and valuable characteristic, a correspondence between objects and humans that not only signifies openness but also addresses the need to respect the interrelationship between material, place, and task. In other words, tolerance is about the power of the real – in two respects, from twin perspectives. It is again about the *poetry* of such moments, whose experiential quality is dependent upon things that preceded us and with which we have nothing to do, but which we should seek to recultivate in a potential design. The latest sociological thinking also refers to such moments and highlights the fundamental importance of this topos for a society that strives for the maximum individual freedom of action. In his widely read book, Hartmut Rosa describes the phenomenon of "resonance" as a concept that is central to our relationship with the world. He links it to the notion of "Unverfügbarkeit" (unavailability). True resonance is only possible in situations in which things are not completely accessible or available: "a relation to the world that knows and allows no interruptions or disturbances, no encounters with the foreign or unfamiliar, no periods of estrangement from oneself and the world, would [...] ultimately fall *mute.* Nothing in the world would remain *inaccessible;* the world would lose its own voice and thus its responsive quality, while the subject would in turn lose his or her capacity to change."[6] It is by resisting the dominant trend towards growth and expediency that we will maintain the ability to resonate that gives our life meaning. The presence that we experience in the things around us is a surrogate for this concept, because it always is: material, spatial, tangible – concrete; because it richly enhances the design process – and can guide this process in very special ways – with its inherent imponderables and diversions, secrets and enclosures, and, indeed, risks and obstacles. We must enter into conversation, into dialog, with the presence of the existing, because this will not only reveal its qualities but also offer us instructions about our own work – about our project.

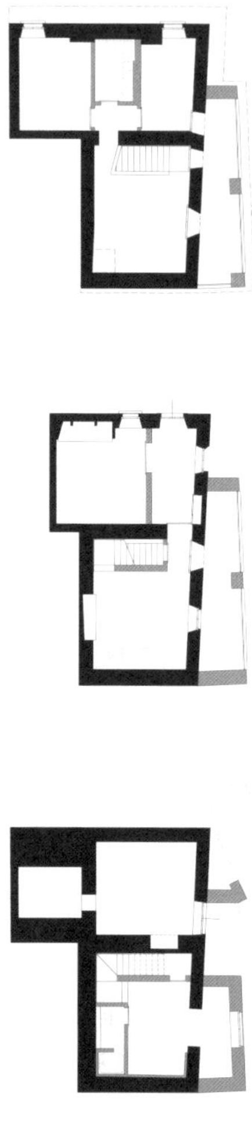

House in Monte, Ticino, roof, ground, and basement levels
Renovation Jonathan Sergison

The House of the Architect

Every opportunity is an offer. Thus begins Jonathan Sergison's account of his fascination for a house in Monte, a mountain village high above Mendrisio in the canton of Ticino. It first caught his eye when he started teaching at the Università della Svizzera italiana. Four years after buying the house in 2010, the approximately 350-year-old structure has become his family home – in summer everyone is here. Sergison speaks of domesticity as the theme of his design interventions. These begin with the retention of the house, not by preserving every trace as building conservation – the act of conserving and protecting historic buildings and other monuments – may demand, because the house is a listed building. But this is not the basis of his meticulous approach. Rather, he was convinced from the very beginning by the presence of history in the form of the spaces and structure of this piece of the jigsaw of the village's built fabric. One could say: It is about the resonance of the inconspicuous. In order to retain this quality, the avowed metropolitan had to find the right use for these spaces, in the heart of a mountain landscape that remains, to this day, as tough as it is idyllic. This landscape sets the tone, defines the way of life, as long as one engages with it. Everything had to remain and, yet, had to change so that the domesticity ingrained in the house by earlier inhabitants could also remain, by becoming a domesticity that corresponds with his family and himself.

When Jonathan speaks of his house, he begins with the views that are possible here, into the spaces, into the streets. Then – when one steps out of the house into this distinctive network of public spaces that permeate the cluster of similar houses in the clearing on the steep mountainside – there is the view of the distant forests on the opposite side of Val di Muggio. Thinly spread and surrounded by forest, the few villages resemble pearls, strung out along the necklace of a narrow and, for the inexperienced, rather dangerous road; the people up here seek to obtain their provisions through exchange, each village offers something. One becomes aware of this after completing the steep climb up into this seemingly isolated world. As it traces its circular route between the villages, this road becomes a communicating vessel, the supply artery of the people of this enticing corner of the Southern Alps, who have no desire to return back down into the valley. The "House in Monte," as it is referred to by the architect from afar who was brought here by his work, is an example of the all-embracing interconnectedness of the local that is possible today. This does not have to involve destruction: It is possible to not just retain such buildings, such places, but also enhance them so that they belong to the present. We are reminded of this by the exotic plants – the palms, citrus trees, camellia, oleander – that have been introduced into the landscape around Ticino's lakes over the course of the past few centuries. They bear witness to the fact that change also brings opportunity – in this sublime mixed climate with the light that suddenly hits you as you enter the Southern Alps. It will not be long before the landscape levels out and heads for the sea.

The house first had to be stabilized structurally, it had been neglected. Following building measures that were as decisive as they were essential, it now appears to have been inserted into its rocky

surroundings – its raw plaster surfaces interacting with its neighbors. But it does not feel set apart, because one senses that this is a building that was already here. We get the strange feeling that we are looking at a doppelganger. Anyone comparing the images of the near ruin of the original building with Hélène Binet's photographs notes the skill with which the former timber outhouse has become today's loggia and sees how it provided the inspiration that has led to something new. But it does not force itself upon us – it does not declare: "I am the work of an architect!" The walled forecourt reinforces the spatial qualities of the old in-between space, holding off the tightly woven urban space of the village and establishing the privacy that we seek today. All the essential elements are based on current needs, but these are subordinate to the permanence of the house and when we find them they almost seem like new "opportunities" that are waiting to be discovered. Such a house, which is inherently rich in quality and has developed slowly as it has passed from hand to hand, offers much to the present: The parlor remains the parlor, because the hearth, the physical manifestation of the open fire, was and remains an essential element. Facing the street, it can also serve today as a study or a formal dining room; here is the newly inserted library. The kitchen is practical, but modestly equipped, and its fittings do not compete with the open fire. This room is a focal point in the labyrinthine layout, a stair climbs from here to the next floor. Thus, the present has been anchored in the historical use of the house, whose spatial implicitness reflects rural daily life, because it is still a place of ritual. And even if the house's earlier role, to accommodate the equipment that enabled farmers to remain self-sufficient, was

different, a certain similarity with today's role remains. A vague sense of *presence* sets in – does this come from me, do I feel as if I have "arrived"? What else should characterize a home? Is it the permanence of the space that generates this sense of presence, this new relationship or ambivalent condition that we cannot master and hence, perhaps for precisely this reason, find so satisfying? This form of reading a space through the continuation of its usages is underpinned by a design principle: to build buildings that unite the qualities of the vernacular, without being traditionalist. In contrast – this is about adaptation through renewal, about reinterpretation based on respecting the limits of the existing.

Inside the house we rediscover the issues raised by the integration of the old-new building volume into the fabric of the village: This is a form of "infill" made from local spruce that is robustly inserted by local artisans into the historical rectangular stone volume and whose only decoration is the unpredictable, natural, and constantly intriguing, eye-catching pattern created by the dark knotholes.
In other words, the crumbling interior of the existing building is re-created like a sheath. Another surprising aspect of this interior is that, for all this respect shown to the characteristics of a place, it is clear that there is an overarching approach, in which "New Building" and "Continued Building" no longer appear to be conflicting categories. This is all Continued Building. Jonathan expresses a similar thought during our morning visit. Later, we reread the project, in order to explicitly identify those principles that have also become built reality in Monte, where they have created a work full of reserve and sensual presence. In a form of theoretical guideline for their own practice, we find this concept of "tolerance" towards the "as

found," a sensibility for the scarcity and beauty of the existing, with which Jonathan Sergison and Stephen Bates anchor themselves in the art and architecture of the Late Modern: "Tolerance indicates an acknowledgement of the found conditions of a situation, in both emotive and physical terms, and an ability to work with and make interpretations of these conditions; informs an approach to construction in which structural solutions accommodate spatial ideas rather than dictate them. The enveloping material then becomes the important element in the expression of space; offers tangible possibilities for connecting spaces and provides systems which enable rather than prescribe use."[7] At the highpoint of the chain of materials, construction, space, and effect, our relationship with the shared "Lebenswelt" (life-world) becomes a reference, a way of allowing oneself to become part of a place.

In a key text, in which he introduced critical regionalism into the wider debate, Kenneth Frampton famously argued for an alliance between the principles of modern building and the qualities of a region as a means of countering an economized architecture that is reduced to "surface." In retrospect – and in view of the many current crises that have been compounded by the loss, both real and symbolic, of valuable "local" knowledge – this approach still has much to offer in such areas as food, energy, and drug production, etc. Frampton argues that we should counter globalization with a model of built differentiation, in which we incorporate precisely those elements that differentiate traditional building methods from globalized ones – the local, concrete, characteristics of a place – into our designs. He can be interpreted as asserting that good design knowingly rejects some of the so-called freedom offered

by the modern world in order to restate the cultural importance of unavailability – "[...] it does offer a critical basis from which to evolve a contemporary architecture of resistance – that is, a culture of dissent free from fashionable stylistic conventions, an architecture of place rather than space, and a way of building sensitive to the vicissitudes of time and climate. Above all, it is a concept of the environment where the body as a whole is seen as being essential to the manner in which it is experienced."[8] Once again, the task of design is to reevaluate the concreteness of the physical – a concreteness that we, as living beings, share with all the objects in a space. In the wake of Modernism and Postmodernism, this modernism is about combining technical universalism and a raised awareness of place and of the need to embrace the given with all the senses. One example of the local universalism that is so effective in Monte is the way in which the lighting mood in the tight fabric of the village was adopted as a way of articulating the sensibility of the place. A window, which is typical for the work of the architect – and which is also used in narrow London courtyards –, draws the light falling onto the sloping roofs into the intimate private space. We find the same window in Stephen Bates's house in Cadaqués: but interpreted in a different way. The impression created by the Mediterranean space is one of stone, whiteness, light, but also coolness in the hot summer. In the Southern Alps, it is a volume made of wood, of spruce, inserted in a stone structure. Jonathan and the artisans use local wood. The only exception is the treaders of the stair. The norms demand that these are made of hardwood and this leads to an essential yet elegant detail. In both places, frugality and simplicity become sensual luxury. Time and time again we are reminded of the wall in the English landscape, their model for authorless, inherent beauty. It is a model that anyone can use if they understand the basic principle: "The use of common and modest material in the making of our projects is a strategy for engaging with the familiar components of everyday situations. The re-use and reconfiguration of familiar materials may promote a re-valuing of things which have previously been taken for granted."[9]

An important lesson can be learned from the model of Monte: One can only execute that which one experiences oneself. There are cultures that have raised everyday culture to a form of high art. It is no surprise that, more than a century ago, the West sought a new elementarity in the ancient cultures of Asia – or in the constructional traditions of the Alps and the Mediterranean. Soetsu Yanagi, the Japanese theorist in the area of artisanship, speaks of ordinary "miscellaneous things," which incorporate this elementarity in an almost ritual manner. One advantage of using artisanship as a model – despite the fact that this restrictive label has Western origins and is untenable in the phenomenological space – is that we do not lose sight of the importance of use. Yanagi tells us of the *zakki*, the traditional Japanese everyday objects, whose innate association with artisanship is based on repetitive use and generates a beauty that is inseparable – a familiarity that can also become *alien.* This combination of the materials and the use of an object, which, in alliance with the senses, remain visible and tangible in the context of doing, brings us back to the issue of freedom and limitation in the sense of tolerance. We cannot design such quality without addressing the question of use.[10] Consequently, there is symmetry in artisanal objects when they both facilitate and embody usage. While

Nikolaus Pevsner was still able to trace a linear trajectory from artisanship to the machine age and its logical conclusion, we have reason to reflect: Architects should reevaluate their role. This is not about dreaming, about offering a voice to a long sidelined group – it is about everyday sensations and the room for maneuver that a culture awards itself; it is not about mere gainful employment but about concrete work that forges relationships. And it is affirmed by the American philosopher Matthew B. Crawford, who speaks of the situatedness of the self in the concrete world that we have to constantly appropriate and that only fully blossoms in "skilled practices. (...) For it is when we are engaged in a skilled practice that the world shows up for us as having a reality of its own, independent of the self."[11] We design not on the basis of our own creativity alone, but from our experience of this reality.

The Phenomenological Dimension

On the level of architectural theory, the Finnish architect Juhani Pallasmaa emphasized the central position of a design method, in which the concreteness of the world of objects influences us as long as our hands and our own physicality remain connected with the act of building – in contrast with the abstraction of the plan and CAD, of norms and images. In an interview, he suggests that built history, existing objects, are nothing other than a "body of sensory knowledge"[12] – while taking a position vis-à-vis the concept of style by describing it as a form of humanistic classification. Even if a building is historical, we experience it in the here and now, as if it never existed detached from our body. All buildings, whether outstanding or ordinary, have taught us to be sentient beings and provided a basis, upon which we can constitute ourselves as physical and spiritual creatures. For Pallasmaa, this includes a plea for the continuity of built reality over time, but also between our bodies and the world – with implications for the concrete work, and the ethos, of design. In his "Six themes for the next millennium," one of the key manifestos of recent architectural theory, he says, fully in the spirit of existential escalation: "Architecture is a conservative art. It is conservative in the sense that it materialises and preserves the history of culture. Buildings and cities trace the continuum of culture in which we place ourselves and by which we can recognize our identities. The way I see the essence of architecture's conservatism does not exclude radicality; on the contrary, architecture must reinforce our existential experience in a radical manner against the forces of alienation and detachment. Architecture, as all art, makes us experience our own being with extraordinary weight and intensity."[13] If one wanted to teach this form of radicalism in an architecture school, one book would be the preferred teaching material – it is an architectural diary of the senses, a very special history book: *Experiencing Architecture,* which is unsatisfactorily translated into German as "Architektur Erlebnis" (Architecture Experience), was published by Steen Eiler Rasmussen in 1957. If history were not dead narrative and architecture were the discipline that brings together those who build, inhabit, and design, lived reality rather than stylistic or hegemonic theory, then we would have to tell stories like Rasmussen as a basis for our designs. Upon reading these stories, experiences are reawakened in phenomenal spaces of shared imagination: The colors of architecture, natural rather than artificial light, textures, physical corpulence, the topography of a city, the smell of a garden, the silence of a room – all this and more is discussed and made tangible via examples of built architecture. Rasmussen has little interest in either styles or the names of architects. Even when telling of a Roman basilica he energetically focuses not on the magnificent interior that tourists would mostly appreciate, but its outside wall and its role in a children's ballgame. Everything in the game seems to be happening for the first time and in a unique way: an intense here and now. While in no way diminishing the great achievements of architecture, Rasmussen seems to suggest that we can only really appreciate it if we first learn to experience its elementary qualities: firmness, space, height, inclination, interaction. Once again, it is down-to-earth and immediate experience that is the decisive reference of architecture as a living environment.

Widely described as phenomenological, this approach will not be explained here in philosophical terms but, rather, as part of architectural history. One of the first attempts to explain phenomenology from the perspective of modern architectural theory, *Experiencing Architecture* was, in a certain sense, expanded upon by Norberg-Schulz and Pallasmaa. It fundamentally addresses the reconciliation between sensuality and the rational order, which not only, clearly, dominates the modern world, but also seeks to resolve the crises of the future.

The essay "Working with Tolerance" is being written by Jonathan Sergison and Stephen Bates at the same moment as Christian Norberg-Schulz, in one of his later texts, is hinting at what the "unvollständige Projekt der Moderne" (unfinished project of modernity) could be, while also appearing, in a certain way, to be exploring the foundations of his theories. It is surprising not only that he is addressing the old subject of reconciling reason and sense, but also that he sees this as so significant for today's architecture – and combines it with the classical modern to establish a new tradition: "The constant credo of Le Corbusier, Gropius and Mies van der Rohe is that architecture is art, but the means that are employed are contemporary technology and functional insight. That the artistic element is emphasised is because of the dominating role played by the intellect since the Age of Enlightenment, with 'feelings' being reduced to a matter of taste. This is still true today [...]. In the sense that [...] man places himself outside things, as an observer, instead of living and interacting with them. We could also say that what had previously been a qualitative thing was reduced to an object. [...] It is not possible here to discuss the 'thingness' of architecture. Let me simply say that every work of architecture is also recognised 'as something' therefore we can say 'tower', 'dome', 'gable', 'doorway', 'window', etc. They are all recognised by their being-in-the-world, or more precisely by how they exist between heaven and earth – in other words, by how they stand, rise up, stretch out, open or close themselves. This always occurs as an actual built form. Architecture is thus the art of building and as such it has the ability to give a house a qualitative presence."[14] For Norberg-Schulz, design is about reconciliation. A new phenomenological architecture has its origins in not only the intentional reconciliation of reason and sense discussed here, but also the reevaluation of situatedness and use in the design process as well as of the question of what concreteness means in the case of objects over which we have no control. The proximity between our understanding of a specific place and what we bring to it is essential and manifests itself in *Gebrauch* (use). A house can be such a place. It is always concrete and presents itself as a design task that is never completed and begins with existing objects. There was also talk of a poetic design approach. This still ranks ahead of terms such as "aesthetic" or "beauty," even if beauty means nothing more than things being in harmony, being together in such a way that their presence *satisfies.* Achieving this would be the primary task of Continued Building in the sense of developing further, which begins not as a scientific, or conservationist, or ecological task, but with the existing substance that enables a presence to be created in this place. A new phenomenology in architecture must seek to refocus our attention on our experience of architecture in our living environment: What it means to be surrounded by walls, to have a view, to feel warm on a cold winter's day, and so on. There is a degree to which the cheerfulness of a color, the rawness of a plaster surface or smoothness of a polished stone, the absorptiveness of wood, the coolness of glass, a glowing reflection or swallowed light, etc. *concerns us* directly. The question is the extent to which we appreciate this, and to which we experience the special in our daily lives.

And hence, the first part of this book is a plea for Continued Building based on the example of a house and how it is used. If the role of design is to present new possibilities and yet, despite this, it has to constantly turn to prior experiences of concrete places where designers and inhabitants meet, then the focus of this process is a specific, everyday encounter with reality. Or, in a way, the dual nature of *revealing* and being *revealed.* And how would the world of objects and its related spaces change if we followed this example? It goes without saying that the Continued Building that is presented here as an obvious basis for designing has little to do with our current professional reality – and yet it can be demonstrated by examples that could become models. Those, for whom the term "phenomenological" appears too philosophical in this context, are referred to the logical assertion by the Viennese architect Hermann Czech that it is simply impossible to define the purpose of a room in advance because this only becomes clear through use, through our own spatial presence. And the bases of this clarity are, once again, previous experiences of the living environment that we, as it were, reencounter in the room of architecture, and the rooting of a project in our shared experience. In contrast with the modern differentiation and professionalisation of architecture, which seems to have relegated the profession to some unique position on the margins of the shared world, we should argue for a transformation that our society will not be able to avoid, whatever form it takes. Namely, society can turn away from its belief in the logic of growth and acknowledge an approach to the existing that is not about honoring dead objects but, rather, searching for possibilities in the wealth of the given. And, when this happens, architecture will only be beginning in the manner in which it should be beginning anyway.

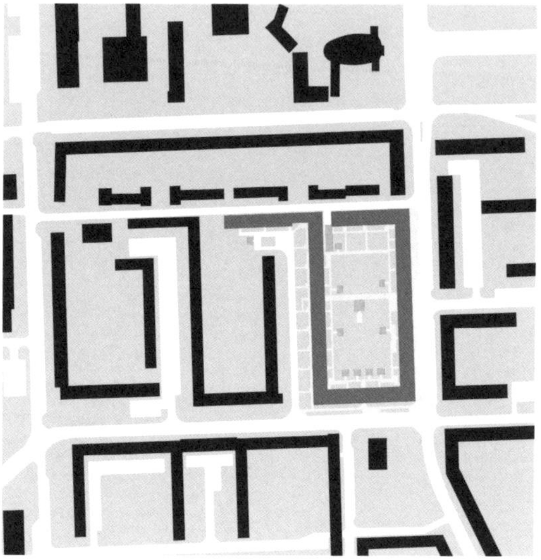

Bindermichl, Linz, location plan
Renovation Franz Riepl

Living Contexts

"The construction of the barns was a sort of moment of renewal in the building of a village, because they kept getting larger and higher. [...] We had two groups of carpenters: The work of one group became more and more pleasing while that of the other became increasingly coarse. I asked myself why this was happening – why, in one case, the structures were becoming more 'graceful' and 'appealing.' Of course these are the wrong words, for the truth is that one was simply delighted that their work was so beautiful. But why didn't the other group manage this?"[15] Questions such as "how is it done?" and "why is the form appealing?" resonate in the memory of the architect – not to forget the delight in experiencing the achievement that echoes in these words. Franz Riepl's meditations about his own introduction to village life touch upon a moment of initiation that occurred when he was still a child. The architect was born. Riepl, who has been a self-employed architect in Munich since 1967 and was Professor of Agricultural Building and Rural Settlement at Graz University of Technology until 2000, remains faithful to these early experiences of the rural area in which he was born in the north of Upper Austria. This is where he first experienced the act of construction in the form of the erection of simple timber structures, and these are the events that he turns to when he later recalls his first conscious contact with building. His career took him from the country to the city and from the village inn and butcher's shop to university, to Vienna and Munich, and to a completely different milieu. His personality can deal with these contrasts, his character allows him to remain mindful – of the world of the middle-class and the bourgeoisie as well as the world of the farmer. He becomes a tireless observer of his environment.

He is constantly returning to a rurality, which appears to be a counter-world yet remains a critical authority when we address today's predominantly urban architecture, a rurality, which we constantly believe to be disappearing, but which stays alive for him because it now accompanies him in his role as an architect. In a certain sense this is the story of Jonathan Sergison in reverse – or it would be if our aim was to exploit the narrative of city and country as antitheses, which ignores the fact that, although we have, and should have, both city and country, we have also long since developed a shared sensibility for the differences between them. Just like we have developed a sensibility for the achievements of the historical cultural landscape and, now, even for the importance of local production under fair conditions for humans, animals, and plants – for the refinement of products that, like the craft of building, are subject to practical constraints. When the people of the village were working together back then, it was not about "architecture." As long as this was the case, such examples of the constantly necessary renewal and rejuvenation remained restrained forms that were integrated into the organism of the village; there, were they had their preordained place in the evolved typology of living and

working for people and animals, of spaces for commerce, calm, and movement. Building a village was also town planning. Achieving something under constraints that both establish the framework and generate forms that renew this framework is a process that will characterize the later work of the architect Franz Riepl. "Überzogen" (exaggerated) is one of the terms that he uses when commenting on the architectural activities that he is constantly, closely observing all around him. Despite his admiration for the regular top performances achieved in contemporary building, he does not consider architecture to be a competitive "high performance sport," in which new forms and paradigms should be generated on a daily basis. At least, not as long as we are able to resolve the everyday tasks of our built environment in an unobtrusive manner or, better still, as long as satisfying and solid things happen anyway, with or without the help of designers.

And yet: Here is an architect who is vigilant about refinement. Franz Riepl, who has long been one of Austria's leading architects of cooperative housing, has applied himself to the design of many things – farmhouses with concrete shells, a stadium, elegant residential buildings, and furniture – and has received many prizes, but refinement is not the word that he turns to in conversation. His work is about the "griffig," the graspable or tangible. This hints at the understanding of life and work of the traditional farming society, a society that was already changing radically during his childhood and from which he stepped back, in order to be able to work on the outside, with distance and closeness – both of which characterize the work of such a designer. He recalls those who were already no longer able to live from farming back then, the so-called "part-time farmers" and "cottagers" who – and Franz Riepl is so matter-of-fact that this never sounds nostalgic – knew how to enhance their lives with a few farm animals and their last remaining bit of land and, rather than surrendering completely to full-time work, more-or-less sustain themselves during their latter years from their knowledge and skills, which were unpaid but invaluable. They might not have been aware of this and their life was not easy, but the model remains interesting today, at a time in which young people are seeking balance, or a life that is not completely dominated by full-time work, and the term "freedom" is up for discussion. For the designer, such tendencies are illustrated by forms of use, by the way in which people live and *set up* their lives.

This has little to do with money and much more to do with a love for things on which people leave the traces that make them theirs. Rural life included lively discussion, sociability, and a devotion to the garden and to objects of daily use. For an engaged architect who is looking back over their life, it seems as if the inhabitant of these perfectly appropriated habitats (which were only left-over spaces in the long-since industrialized agricultural landscape) is a Gesamtkunstwerk. Their conversation covers spatial experiences: It addresses the interdependencies of an Upper Austrian parlor, often found in the corner of a building; the magnificent light, pouring in from two sides, marking the passage of the day in an interior space in which one works or rests or sits together, whether this is the parlor of the inn or the farmhouse. This is one of the phenomena that accompanied Franz Riepl during the duller moments of his studies. And then there were the discussions in the inn; about how it was done, about how someone else did it better. Architecture was building and a subject of general debate, because it was a common task, and because everyone built, supported by artisans: "The thing that fascinated me as a child: the fact that something emerges, that something is built, that suddenly a building is standing there!" The creation of space for ourselves is the elementary origin of architecture, and this fascination remains to this day. At university, he learnt about the sober modernism of the post-war years, which thoroughly suited the pragmatism of the country boy, who was required to rapidly empathize with the international architecture world just as Josef Frank and the Vienna School were starting to be rediscovered in the capital. Franz Riepl has particularly fond memories of his teacher, Friedrich Lehmann. Lehmann gave courses in which building typologies came alive – and this appears to be the first hint of something that has gone on to characterize all the architect's work and which may even represent its secret core, whether it is a piece of furniture with a Danish air, a large factory, or a residential block: the search for the "qualities of use," which the budding architect can only truly find in buildings, in existing fabric, in spaces, movements, paths, gestures, human glances, rituals, materials, and voices – in the atmospheres of banks, hotels, and theaters, from which he learns to understand that he first has to experience something before he can, perhaps, also design it.

But design itself, the sacred cow of architectural education, is a subject about which Franz Riepl continues to say very little to this day; he speaks about architecture – but only when asked about his own buildings –, pursues it, visits landscapes and buildings, speaks to people about them, and this leads to something: buildings. And thus, "bauen" (to build) has probably remained the more important idea for him. Everything that architecture is about comes together in the built object. However, as Riepl is an architect who, while avoiding theoretical writing, not only intensively moves around and observes his surroundings, but also passes on his critical conclusions and suggestions in countless letters to fellow citizens, politicians, colleagues, and the media, this is a further indication that his work does not end with the concrete project but also continues in the never finished process of building, which includes more than the design of an object. This is exemplified by ongoing personal relationships with his best clients: This exchange is mutual. Those who get to know him better will eventually get the chance to visit the Krennmayrs. He "restored" the Dambachmayrhof in Kematen, a wonderful example of a Vierkanter – a farmhouse built around a courtyard –, a sort of "fortress" in the gently rolling landscape close to the Danube, for the farming couple over a ten-year period starting in the mid-1970s. The contact has remained ever since, there are always small jobs that need doing, and the house is now in the hands of the next generation. Here, restoration means: restructuring the farm without conspicuously affecting its appearance (these are refinements), improving the heights of the spaces while retaining their scale and the important vaulting, and, at the same time, addressing the rigor of rural life by introducing a little of the coziness that one would expect of a home in the town. Not, however, that this is out of place because, while building a house in which people continue to work and live under the same roof and that presents the farmer and his wife with a way of life that they adopt and adapt to and make their own, Franz Riepl learns how to spatially remodel such a farm so that it enables one to farm well and also be able to afford this life – step-by-step, and always in line with the wellbeing of the animals. In other words, these things go hand in hand, new ways of working and new ways of living and, because this architecture is a dialogic process, everything has assumed a form that seems to have already been there. Which, of course, it has.

The Content of the Form

The view in the historical aerial photograph from 1954 stretches far beyond an Upper Austrian Vierkanter. Behind, we see a monumental form that resembles the white bones of an unknown creature: the quadrangles, the comb-like spreading wings and blocks of a large, multistory housing complex that is bordered, on the south, by the Hummelhofwald, which is now a recreation area for the provincial capital of Linz. The landscape collides with a new settlement, which recalls the typology of the typical farmhouse due to the fact that the huge form is named after the farm that had to make way for its construction. Fifteen long years have passed since March 1939, when the city in which Adolf Hitler went to school, the capital of the Gau of Oberdonau, was named one of the five Führer cities. The city has the potential to be more than just the Führer's place of retirement – as Reichsbaurat, Roderich Fick is given responsibility for the construction of the monumental city center on the right bank of the Danube before, later, Hermann Giesler assumes the delicate role. The industrial city of Linz is to expand to more than double its former size and almost quadruple its population. Not just heavy industry but also housing – and the construction of housing estates – is responsible for this expansion between 1938 and 1945. To the southeast of the old town and to the west of the industrial areas and the river, with its port and huge concentration of rail tracks, in the heart of this new residential quarter, we find the Wohnhof Am Bindermichl. The housing complex is the work of Herbert Rimpl, who was born in Silesia and trained in Munich in the 1920s. Significantly influenced by Theodor Fischer, for whom he worked before becoming familiar with Augsburg's mixture of modern and traditional as cultivated in Bavaria's *Postbauschule* under Robert Vorhoelzer, his Heinkel aircraft plant in Rostock-Marienehe causes a sensation and brings him into contact with the armament efforts of National Socialism. He comes to the attention of the Head of the Aviation Ministry. Between 1937 and 1945, Rimpl runs the building department of the government factories that bear the name of Hermann Göring. With his staff of up to 200 he designs residential complexes and industrial plants in many locations. His projects in Upper Austria's provincial capital include the Spallerhof, the Makarthof, and, naturally, Bindermichl. He builds for people and machines. His buildings feature both modern forms and pitched roofs, dutifully separated depending upon the typology.

The overall program consists of 7,000 apartments for 30,000 people, including 1,400 in Bindermichl, the construction of which begins in 1940. Despite the monumentality of the multistory blocks, the detailing is serial and sober: perforated facades, box-type windows, gateways, arched passages, offset windows in the staircase, pragmatism. But this is urban planning that still falls back on old principles. Supervised by Albert Speer, the central axis, next to the motorway feeder, should accommodate not only the workers from the government factories and migrants. The four-story blocks facing the main road are more prestigious and urban, with narrow balconies, stone bases, and a sprinkling of sculptural detail. These were earmarked for doctors, lawyers, and salaried employees, while the workers lived on the streets behind. The central area, with its shops and public buildings, surrounded by the housing blocks of

Bindermichl, remained empty and, although everything had come to a halt in 1944, Linz's post-war socialists resume the housing program of the Nazi Era and reuse the partly bomb-damaged so-called "Hitler Buildings." Due to the shortages of the post-war years, the open spaces become fields or remain, as envisaged by Nazi ideology, vegetable gardens. Self-sufficiency is not a new issue, neither is the autonomous wood burner. As prosperity increases, the buildings are upgraded; the outside walls are insulated, new double glazing meets the norms but leads to the loss of the timber windows, whose fine glazing bars adorned the facades. Finally, lift towers are built.

For most of the incomers, the generally austere two-room apartments with their own toilet and bathroom signified an improvement in their living conditions. They now belong to WAG, Wohnungsanlagen GesmbH, for whom Franz Riepl often worked. He set new standards there and sought to use the funding that politicians occasionally approved for improvements that built upon the basically good substance – in close dialog with the heads of the former large cooperative. He repeatedly demanded more resources so that social housing could achieve what it was capable of. Bindermichl is, in many ways, a model and the ultimate manifestation of his energetic ambition to improve the housing conditions of the less prosperous. It is a lesson in Continued Building, in an area in which this is much needed – the improvement of buildings that many regard as politically questionable and with which few readily identify. Riepl, in contrast, who also applied the principles of Continued Building to, for example, the Makarthof for WAG, has constantly succeeded in transforming these blocks, the repetitiveness of whose facades is regarded by many as ideological, into buildings that are full of char-

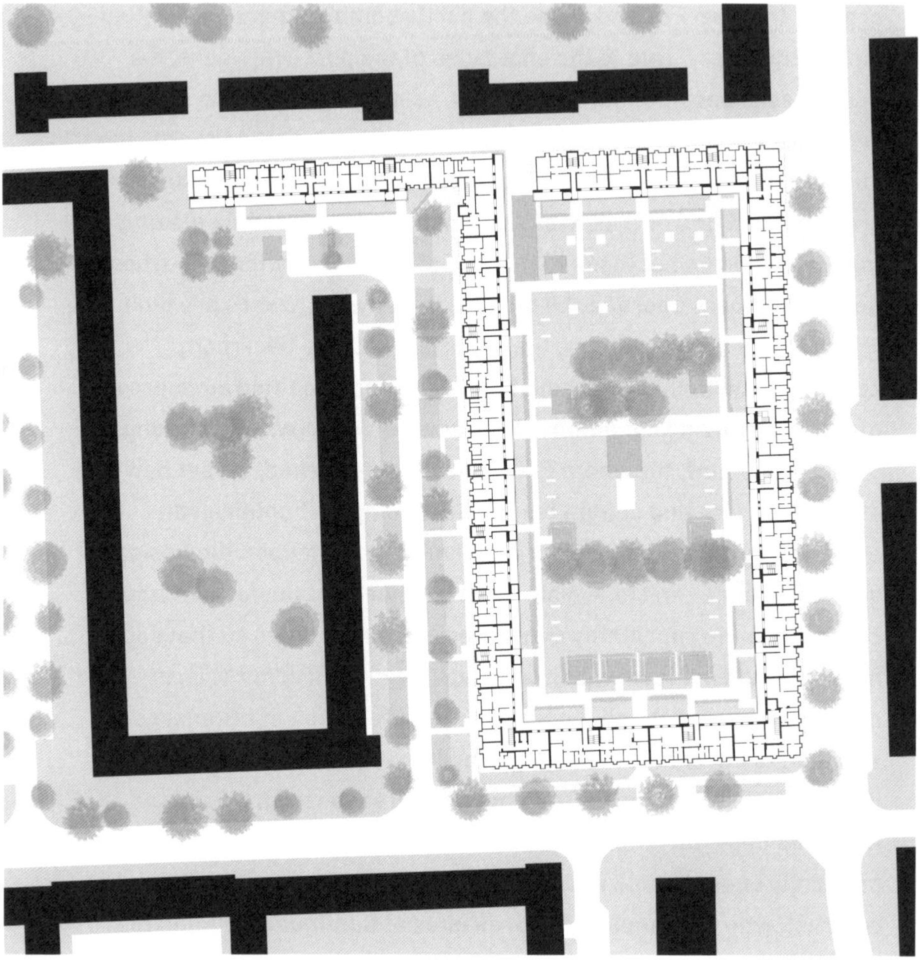

Bindermichl, Linz, new roof level apartments
Renovation Franz Riepl

acter – using constructional means: wall surfaces, the forms and depths of windows, rhythm, good proportions, good detailing (often in steel), balconies, protective elements, additions, and extensions. This work demands that artisans are guided until it is clear what is required, even though this certain something is often so incidental that the architect has not even needed to involve his client.

The then 88-year-old Franz Riepl should not even have been awarded the Bindermichl project. Around 20 years ago he sought to add balconies to the building. The idea came to nothing. But now lifts should be added and, due to his earlier thorough analysis of the structure, he is the only person who can supply usable plans that show the building in its current configuration. So he gets to work. He bases his intervention on two premises that appear to counter the requirement that the complex, in line with the current trend, should be densified. On the one hand, the demand for greater efficiency must not lead to the loss of the generous open space of the courtyard that could enhance the residential qualities of the ensemble. And on the other hand, he has no intention of distancing himself from the existing building in order to send an aesthetic signal and create a dubious stir – as exemplified by the way in which many refurbishment projects by colleagues lead to the loss of distinctive roof landscapes. Hence, the architect places a reinforced and raised pitched roof on the old-new building and, by hardly changing the inclination, creates an extra level with around 50 apartments with floor-ceiling heights of about three meters. And in the courtyard, where he positions a new volume containing the required and requested lift towers, he also creates – in a "buffer zone" resulting from the new roof geometry – terraces and a new spatial layer containing loggias. The building is now oriented to the courtyard. These interventions, which, though few in number, transform the identity of the building, are the result of a lengthy struggle – the lifts should be free-standing and separated from the building as usual because the two-room apartments will otherwise require too many costly lifts with double doors and, hence, the loggias should be replaced by continuous walkways – but the eventual winner is the solution sought by the architect: the unity of the building. Once again, technical pragmatism becomes architecture. This is true Continued Building – the creation of space rather than the addition of technology.

The southeast section of Bindermichl, a courtyard of approximately 200 x 100 meters, is very different from the rest of the quarter upon completion in 2020. The new spatial layer, around two meters in depth, decisively improves the residential quality – but the overall historical form has been so assiduously retained that only the freshly painted facade and skylights hint at the changes within the block. The owners felt that it was unnecessary to spend more. Hence, the street facade appears little changed, even if the apartments behind it have turned around to face the courtyard, which has remained green. By being asked to choose between doors and windows for the wall between the apartment and the loggia, the residents were able to decide for themselves how they would access their newly created private open space. And they did not have to move out, they remained in their homes during the construction work – and afterwards, too. The most impressive aspect of the transformation of this social housing complex using the simplest constructional means is the replacement of its former air of sobriety and, in the eyes of some,

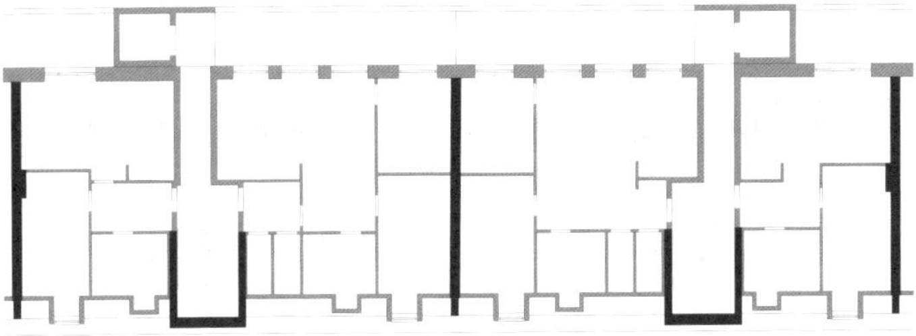

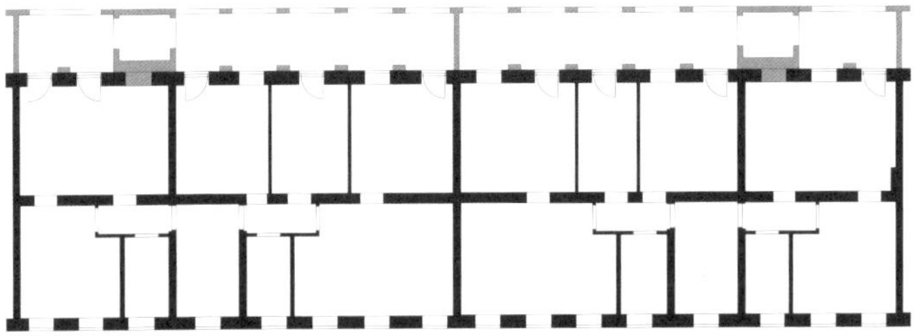

Bindermichl, Linz, new roof level; standard level with loggias
Renovation Franz Riepl

even sadness by a sense of serenity or, indeed, timelessness. This achievement was far from self-evident, given the minimum room for maneuver left by the brief, the financial resources, and the norms etc., and the sense of calm and composure generated by no more than this layer of perpendicular rectangles – the facade screen with its rhythmic loggia openings –, the white plaster, and the "functional" zone, with its structuring, cubic-abstract lift towers, offers an ironic contrast to the formal excesses of much creative architecture. The many individual apartments seem overcome, almost with a sense of pride, by this huge, monolithic, built form; the residents have a home that meets today's demand for a relationship with an *open space*. On one of his many site visits, Franz Riepl says that a "living understanding of architecture" requires a "structuring idea" that enables us to concretely address the latest functional demands. This does not mean that we should only listen to practical "obligations" if we want to create an "atmosphere" and ensure fitness for purpose with only modest resources. Other "functional demands" may generally provide the basis of such Continued Building, but use itself is also transformed by the quality of a space. If we are sensitive enough, atmosphere becomes an instrument of reception and conception: "Stimmungswerte" (atmospheric values), as Riepl calls them, should be "translated" for the task in question using artistic and artisanal tools.

Regarding atmosphere, Bindermichl is now a role model for form as politics. Or, put another way, for the politics of form. Originally built as a truly monumental block that offered homes to the masses, the complex has been transformed: The once stiff streetfront apartments now face the verdant courtyard and their inhabitants

L 644 VV

can move freely and unrestricted in the shadows of their loggias. The large form may be almost unchanged, but even this severity has been softened as it highlights the tension between the individual and society in a completely different way – as an architectural issue, as it can be examined in postmodernist France or in the social housing built in Vienna between the wars. Here it is the power of just one spatial layer that completely changes the impression of the building – without, however, hiding its historical, built logic: The openings of the internal facade follow the rhythm of the former perforated facade, resulting in a subtle proportional displacement that generates a dynamic structure, which, far from being irritating, is refreshing and attracts attention. This creates an anonymous and yet personalized image, behind which the residents can both develop and conceal their own idea of home. Hence, the complex has received a facade that is idiosyncratic and inimitable, pragmatism in the form of architecture. "City without and country within," says the architect. "Durchgrünung" – as achieved by design and nature, working together – is another term that Franz Riepl often uses and has borrowed from the local Vierkanter and from building that is closely tied to the landscape: Surrounded by fruit trees and gardens, these nestle in – are part of – the rolling cultural landscape. House and courtyard, garden and orchard, meadow, then field, then forest – this is the logic of this cultural landscape, in which the house is embedded. The same applies to the courtyard of Bindermichl, with the circular path that runs along the hedge, the green roofs to the bicycle and bin stores, the central communal pavilion (on the site of its wooden predecessor) in the form of a basilica that, despite this typology, is built from steel in the sober manner of Franz Riepl,

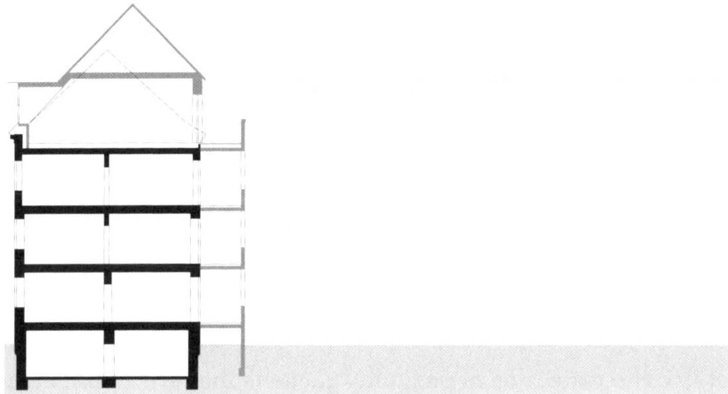

Bindermichl, Linz, section through building showing roof level conversion and new loggias
Renovation Franz Riepl

well-proportioned and with finely-crafted details. The old ash trees have been retained! The broad green lawn provides a place to relax.

The garden recalls the cooperation between Kay Fisker and Gudmund Nyeland Brandt at the Hornbækhus in Copenhagen in 1923. In Linz, the layers are arranged thus: loggia, buffer zone, hedge, path, functional space, lawn, and trees. There is a feeling of elegance. The qualities of the white buildings are only truly revealed by the retained green space. Due to the breadth of the view and the freedom of the courtyard, whose predecessor could be found in a fin-de-siècle courtyard in Graz or any other large Austrian city. Here, however, the many gardens have been combined in a single space, a space owned by the community and, hence, dominated by a sense of generosity. Everyone can share, and enjoy, the view. We do not find the collection of unsightly gardens that are common to many new residential buildings and that invariably bemuse passersby. The same applies to the facade because it is free of overly revealing balconies. A liberal society of individuals, bound together through the form of a building that seeks anonymity in its own way rather than being reduced to an ideologized mass, can now enjoy a home that has been transformed by the soothing simplicity of its form and its green space.

Participation

The example of Bindermichl underlines the extent to which, for Franz Riepl, architecture is building – a never-ending interaction with evolved "usages." He challenges himself to address intrinsic ideas about life, not only because these determine our lives and how we live them, but also because architecture must emerge from the spaces of our living environment: "The best thing for me is when they are filled with a certain experiential delight,"[16] he says, describing his objective.

The second built model for this plea for Continued Building in architecture clearly operates at a different urban scale and is limited in its ability to address specific personal preferences. But this does not alter the role of the architect's awareness of our living environment as the starting point of the design process. In the Linz example, architectural refinement is illustrated by the search for a "mittleres Maß," a benchmark for an architecture that heightens our experience of the elementary in the everyday, but also by the attention paid to tension and the investigation of the tolerances of the existing, which underlie this new form of residential building – in Monte, on the other hand, it was the limitations of the concrete place and the positive identity of the house that had to be retained per se.

This measured atmosphere that is sought and achieved by Franz Riepl hardly features in current architectural theory and, hence, architecture itself. But there is a comparison, albeit one that Riepl himself certainly would not draw and is primarily based on the

conceptual background of such formal expression: Anyone who, upon studying the courtyard facade of Bindermichl, with its intriguing simplicity or even "classicity," its fascinating plasticity, and its dynamic tension, is reminded of the buildings of classical modernism and could well even think of Adolf Loos, whose work famously both shocked and fascinated his contemporaries.

Loos was an exponent of the beneficial atmosphere and a defender of principles. In rural settings, where he was also active when not building amongst the monuments of imperial Vienna, he famously urged architects not to follow the superficial whims of countryside-loving city dwellers, but to investigate the background, the material and constructional bases, to this longing: "Don't build picturesquely. Leave such effects to the cliffs, the mountains and the sun,"[17] he wrote in 1913, 110 years ago, in one of his rules for rural building, which naturally still apply, everywhere. When Loos demanded that we investigate the material and constructional bases to things as a means of ensuring that we only opt for change when this also brings improvement, these are the words of Loos the analyst. But the other side for him is the atmosphere – of both the country and the city. Riepl's thoughts and works have assimilated both lines of argument.

For Loos, being able to live within a culture and without attracting attention was a quality. Culture is a question of shared aspirations and opportunities. But one must also be aware of which things are at their very best in which place: For him, it is the tailors in London and the plumbers in the USA ... and, in Vienna, the culture of the coffee house. We go there and fit in or stand out (if we have to) but, if our objective is Continued Building, we design in line with what we have experienced. Here, too, the central objective is to find the synthesis of form and life, which is known as *atmosphere*. In Loos's own words: "Architecture arouses sentiments in man. The architect's task, therefore, is to make those sentiments more precise. The room has to be comfortable; the house has to look habitable [...]. The architect can only achieve this if he establishes a relationship with those buildings which have hitherto created this sentiment in man."[18] This is also not so dissimilar from the autobiographical reports of Franz Riepl, who adopted this approach in Vienna as part of his professional understanding, and for whom it was very welcome, because he had already understood it in a similar sense outside the professional context, when watching that building work in his home village.

When we speak in architecture of "atmosphere," we soon arrive at Peter Zumthor and his notable use of this word. But what has the master of the intensified spatial experience to do with everyday Continued Building? With a theory of Continued Building based on the holistic architectural experience, as focused on in the first part of this book and then again in the example of Bindermichl? Zumthor – if you listen to him – also follows Loos's example. He begins with a black and white photograph – this time of a Zurich coffee house, captured for us in 1936, a smoke-filled room full of the light of a past and yet present day, words hang between the people, silently filling the place for us. When Peter Zumthor poses the most fundamental questions of his milieu, he speaks of the "Magic of the Real" and appears impressed by the impact of this constructed yet anonymous space: "Men, just sitting around – and they're enjoying themselves, too. And I ask myself, can I achieve that as an architect – an atmosphere like that, its intensity, its mood. And if so, how do I go about it?"[19] Once again, the architect's work begins with a question that identifies the special in the ordinary and stylizes actions as rituals, as customs, as a way of perceiving them more clearly. In order to account for the relationship between his experiences and his profession, he too enters the spaces of the built world – and observes.

What attracts his attention? What does he notice? "Here I am, sitting in the sun. A grand arcade – long, tall, beautiful in the sunlight. The square offers me a panorama – the facades of houses, the church, the monuments. Behind me is the wall of the café. Just the right number of people. A flower market. Sunlight. Eleven o'clock. The opposite side of the square in the shade, pleasantly blue. Wonderful range of noises, conversations nearby, footsteps on the square, on stone, birds, a gentle murmuring from the crowd, no cars, no engine sounds, occasional noises from a building site. I imagine the start of the holidays making everybody walk more slowly."[20] Architecture as a stream of consciousness.

As he then turns, in this well-known lecture "Atmospheres," to the starting point of architecture, Zumthor seeks to explain to his audience that everything that cannot be fully explained can probably still be remembered, because a curious thing about the memory is its ability to clarify and intensify – and it also belongs to the realm of existing things. As he concludes his presentation of his design principles, he specifically speaks of "transcendent levels" and seeks to capture the essence of his role in two appendices on the subjects of "Architecture as Surroundings" and "Coherence." The first addresses the ability of buildings to become part of their anonymous wider environment while the second describes how form, place, and use come together in a way that not only satisfies us but also inspires us to observe and experience. In his architectural practice, Zumthor has known exactly how to intensify these qualities. The special moment is the focal point of his architecture. And he finds these moments in everyday life. Filtering the atmosphere from the ordinary and then reinforcing it; perhaps this is his doctrine, because he associates himself in his open-hearted lecture with Peter Handke's words "Ich lebe nur von den Zwischenräumen" (I only live from the in-between spaces), which are perhaps the significant places on the basis of which we all recount our lives.

The philosopher Emanuele Coccia recently attracted attention with the book *Sinnenleben,* in which he describes, from the perspective of philosophy and cultural sciences, an ongoing shift in our relationship with the world, in which concreteness and immediacy are gaining a new role, which Christian Norberg-Schulz described in his first chapter as the reconciliation between thinking and feeling, and which Peter Zumthor conceals in his built memories, but which is generally absent in design approaches to the world of concrete objects: "We consider ourselves to be rational beings, who think and speak, although, for all of us, life means seeing, tasting, touching, and smelling the world,"[21] is Coccia's analog explanation of the center of the world in *Sinnenleben.* But if Zumthor seeks refuge in "transcendent levels," if the relationship between our senses and our bodies is being reinvented, and if the existing fabric is not "dead" but has a relationship with us that is very much alive – how can we draw more solid conclusions for our design

work? These could be found in the relationship between "closeness" and "distance." Dagobert Frey potentially helps us here – while also trying to explain the position of architecture amongst the arts.
In attempting to explicitly overcome the old duality of space and structure, he creates a starting point for a phenomenological approach. In his still pivotal lecture from 1923, when architectural space and philosophical phenomenology are already part of the theoretical debate, the Viennese art historian resolves the dispute between the two sides in his own way. Could it be the newly "discovered" space – its psychological effect or its construction, whether in the sense of engineering or the Vitruvian order – that constitutes architecture? The key to architecture is that it is the art form that turns people into "participants," he writes in his "Wesensbestimmung der Architektur" (Determination of the Nature of Architecture).

It is no coincidence that this reminds us of Schiller's definition of children's play as the highest form of human freedom. Architecture is precisely the "functional" form that invites participation, rather than deterministically fixing a "purpose." Because the purpose that architecture necessarily pursues always complies with a "certain idea of life," a "will" that we can define ourselves, as Frey explains a couple of lines later. This conclusion is modern and topical, because it recognizes the individual and their needs – practical, social, etc. – but defines them in the context of their environment and fellow humans; as belonging, one could say, to a concrete place. In any event, one would like to interpret this lecture today as an intervention from outside in the debate about the role of architecture and about how it is looking for its place in society, a place between technology and progress, series and abstraction. However, a further feature is central to the definition of architecture. Frey speaks of the possibility of "isolation" in everyday events and architectural space. It is architecture that permits this space to be perceived as such – but not like a painting that hangs before us, whether in a museum or on the wall of a home. Regarding the material concreteness that appears in space as a result of it being used, he adds: "In architecture, on the other hand, material is, in the sphere of aesthetic observation, reality, is itself an aesthetic object. It represents nothing and, much more, it represents itself, is the thing that is represented."[22] We are reminded of Peter Zumthor's concern and Franz Riepl's living memories – or, concretely, of Loos, who, in his text "On Thrift" had already expressed a sensibility for the sensual materiality of the world that is so central to Coccia by stating, almost imploringly: "Material must be deified again. Materials are nothing less than mysterious substances. We should be deeply and reverentially astonished that anything of the kind was ever made."[23] We "feel with the material" he continues. If we consider the design practices that are made possible by this, we can go further: Participation allows us to pause and reflect in a space that exists and then becomes an action, which can detach itself while still remaining part of the whole, in a *form,* that is nothing other than continuation. By its very nature, architecture not only presents itself as subservient, but also, at the same time, claims to be art and, more than this, an art, whose essence is to show things as they are. And, where new architecture is created, this same – more or less coherent – experienced context of understanding remains. The design process tests the options presented by the qualities on offer. It is this that is the true challenge.

So where is the space of this context of understanding – a space in which we are and from which we then leave – other than in the realm of "existing things," which always contains an impulse for developing further? One can better understand the power of this idea by contrasting it with the currently widespread "academic" notion of design, which believes that one must always create something "special" from the outset. The *flow* of our embeddedness in things, which results when we do not separate experiencing from doing and when the world comes together in a common place, is highly auspicious. We have all experienced this, but it is generally obscured by another notion of the everyday in which this experience is still embryonic. In other words, our task is to design on the basis of our understanding of the atmospheres that we experience. Franz Riepl's architecture achieves this through its pursuit of the mittleres Maß – its conscious "refinement towards the tangible."

Hence, Bindermichl is not only a further model, a plea that we address the tasks that directly surround us, but also the highpoint of around sixty years of architectural practice. It is the center of gravity of a pendulum that is able to strike out and master a wide range of building tasks, each with its own coherent solution. However, this so-called "built" center, Riepl's carefully crafted architecture of the everyday experience, is anything other than a means of sedation, calming, or self-satisfaction, but, rather, the general starting point, which we can understand as a concentrated form of that distancing process that enables us to see the elementary, on the basis of which Continued Building becomes possible – as long

as we "return" to it. This is perfectly illustrated by a quote from Franz Riepl's fellow Upper Austrian Adalbert Stifter. In the famous "Preface" to his *Motley Stones,* he writes that: "[...] it is always in people's ordinary everyday infinitely recurring actions that this law most surely forms the fulcrum, for these actions are the lasting the underlying ones, like the millions of fibrils of tree life."[24]

Urban quarter "One" and center of Gallneukirchen, location plan
Architect Max Dudler

Designing the Context

Is it not the duty of those who conserve historical monuments to accept – and to assume responsibility for the Continued Building of – the existing? Is it not they who have the best access to the relevant knowhow? The two buildings discussed above would have corresponded perfectly with a pre-modern understanding of historical conservation – before a modern approach to history drove a division between "monuments" and the rest of the built world and turned them into historical witnesses that act as material messengers of the past. But this is just one side. Because there is a good reason for "conserving" buildings of general interest, for "integrally" retaining them, with all their material traces. Their "authenticity" transforms them into built documents, spaces from the past in the present, differentiates them from chimeras. Then, in a special way, monuments are places where we experience a historical living environment.
But even amongst those few buildings that can truly be considered as first-class monuments, complete preservation is, for obvious reasons, not possible. Life has changed and time does not stand still. Hence, the long-matured vocabulary, the practical knowledge of building conservation, is important for Continued Building, which is also historical conservation today – because it involves precisely

those buildings that really should be preserved, albeit in another way. When conservation and architecture address existing buildings, they should not do so from two different perspectives, particularly as, in practice, they are dependent upon each other. Furthermore, this underlying differentiation is also questionable. For it implies that our built heritage and the knowledge and experience contained therein, is an elitist concern. It hands over decisions about the fate of buildings to officials and encourages us to underestimate the ordinary, personal scale: the fundamental value of spatial presence and precedence for our buildings and our lives, which lies at the heart of this book. In this sense, the borders between the professions, between building and conservation, are far less clear, especially when one considers not only that even monuments age, but also that they have to satisfy us today and, consequently, meet today's requirements in terms of both functional and sensual quality. In addition to this, our understanding of what is a monument has long since changed and now covers every sort of building and building ensemble. Ostensibly, historical knowhow and artisanship is apparent in buildings of the past – for good or ill – which means that "old" does not have to mean "outdated," especially when we consider today's crises and ask if economic progress and technology are not more the problem than the solution and whether stubbornly looking forwards is actually the right thing to do.

In any event, by addressing the commonalities between altering and protecting existing buildings, we also touch upon the extremely important "rational level" at which we have to approach buildings worthy of protection when we begin working on them. At this point, building conservation has an elaborate set of rules, graded according to the level of intervention, which governs our work with the existing with the aim of protecting all that is valuable. This requires knowledge before we can act further. On the basis of this, the work of those who conserve buildings covers the spectrum from simple repair to the highly controversial reconstruction that, for many, has nothing to do with conservation. But there are also heritage values – that range from artistic via cultural to urban planning aspects – to which we can turn in order to visualize what we are really dealing with. These are all ways of rationalizing a task that are necessary in order to understand it – which we often cannot do if we address it too hastily, especially if we do not have the knowhow on which to base our appreciation. In other words, in order to take the right action we must be able to encounter, in a conscious and precise way, what we may have "felt" but could have easily ignored. While this may seem obvious, it is important to emphasize from the phenomenological perspective. This brings us back to today's multilayered and often abstract design process, which is highly likely to introduce distance between one's own experience and the object that is to be built in the future. The same lessons apply here: If we only address monuments from a distance, as distant achievements of another culture, or if we only identify with them as historical documents, then this approach is inadequate, the lessons of these monuments will largely be lost, and, in the worst case, either they will become objects for entertaining tourists or we will end up preserving a culture that is alien because it has ceased to exist. When architecture engages with conservation (caring for the existing) and with the present of a (still) historical building and shows that the present is still subject to the values embodied by this building because it still "moves" us, then building conservation sounds like a specific set of design instructions that remain valid, even if the necessary intervention involves larger scale transformations or buildings that are not listed.

The following rules align design with a thoughtful approach to existing buildings. Martin Boesch, who is both an architect and an expert in building conservation, has set out the steps of such an approach: "Rule 1: Strengthen the identity of the existing building. Rule 2: First seek the answer to every question in the catalog of elements and rules governing the architecture of the existing building. Rule 3: If point 2 provides no answer then this is to be developed from the inner logic of the architecture of the existing building. Rule 4: Exceptions require arguments. [...] Rule 5: Doubt is our true companion [...]."[25] Here, Continued Building is neither subjectivistic design nor strict conservation but, rather, wise interpretation that is not free of doubt. The fact that this does not restrict creativity is demonstrated by the models in this book. The thing that always counts is the existing, which we as a society share and respect because it guides us. While Martin Boesch primarily emphasizes constructional logic, the heritage values in phenomenological Continued Building are the values stored in the building, which reflect not just bygone lives but also our own lives and experiences: shared, concretely, in situ. The above-mentioned interpretation then takes the form of a "sensual reading" of the existing, whether it is a building, a place, a space, or a fragment. It is derived from the wealth of experiences that are to be discovered in the existing substance and that a design can tap into – together with the ruptures that it has also registered. Hans-Georg Gadamer once highlighted the hermeneutics of our understanding of time by speaking of the "constant interaction between our aims in the present and the past to which we still belong."[26] In doing so, he is pointing to the affinity of our living environment with tradition, which undermines the simple stylistic templates of the sort that proliferated in the nineteenth century as political turmoil spread and became ever more serious but have nothing to do with Continued Building. Hence, a further value that is decisive for the phenomenological continuity of time, space, and experience is a sensibility to the alien – in line with the congruence between an awareness of the past and a search for authenticity that still united architecture and building conservation at the beginning of the modern era. This brings us to a series of potential strategies for combining the alien and the familiar in a work of architecture: "Pragmatism" (Lacaton & Vassal), "Constructivism" (Caminada), "Proportionality" (Asplund), "Layering" (Chipperfield), "Sublimation" (Scarpa), "Analogy" (Hild), "Mimesis" (Miller & Maranta), "Alienation" (Šik), "Concretization" (Döllgast), "Inspiration" (Zumthor) – or whichever other name may be given to Continued Building. Its concrete form only emerges "caso per caso." The awareness of modernity is thus brought up to date by the opportunity to activate, rather than adhere to, methods and forms of building: The repertoire of architecture is collective and, by spanning the ages, grants us a new present.

However, one would not seek to strengthen identity, the principle of Martin Boesch's Rule 1, at a distance and using abstract means. Not only is identity a difficult subject, but it also tends to represent a set of relationships. We find it in the category of "Place" (Christian Norberg-Schulz) and also in the work of the founder of Deep Ecology, the Norwegian philosopher Arne Naess. He, on the other hand, speaks of an act of identification as part of the "self-realization of others:" The eighth basic principle of the Deep Ecology Movement combines the possibility of an (ecological) transition with a basic transformation of our living conditions, which requires voluntary resistance to the dominant quantitative debate of technical-industrial capitalism (growth, competition, CO_2 & co.). Once again, the benchmark for this transformation would be our own experiences, which enable us to grow in ourselves. And the setting for the transformation would be our immediate living environment, which, from the perspective of Deep Ecology, includes not only the local community of a historically evolved living environment, with all its objects, spaces, settlements, and landscapes, but also our interdependency with all the living beings that have grown alongside us; and this applies equally to both modern and traditional societies. "Dwelling in situations of intrinsic value,"[27] writes Naess, perfectly expressing this state of sensual appreciation.

"Let us spend our lives in conceiving then,"[28] famously declared Henry David Thoreau more than a century ago in another appeal for the contemplation of the present. This brings us to not only the openness to experience that we have repeatedly addressed in these pages, but also a debate about the qualities that these experiences reveal to us and that we want to continue, and about which we must therefore agree – a debate that also urges us to understand the living environments of other living beings, because these enrich us too. The diversity and richness of such a "genuine experience," which is central to Naess's *Ecosophy,* represents a form of deeper knowledge that is rooted in the ordinary. We have abandoned our narrow focus on use and purpose in favor of immediacy: We grow with others.

This digression via an approach to the ecological basics and measures that is very different to the approach taken by today's compartmentalized professions and social groups brings two central aspects of building conservation into play: care and harmony. In this context, it is hardly surprising that one of the key theorists of modern building conservation used the term "atmosphere" in 1889, in one of the first texts to address the issue. For Alois Riegl, this embodies the central cognitive quality of modern art, because people look to concrete objects for support in the face of the existential challenges of a contingent world.[29] In his *Moderne Denkmalkultus*[30] from 1903, and possibly mindful of the affective concreteness of an atmosphere, he introduces his profession to the concept of "Alterswert," the quality conferred by aging. For Riegl and his followers in the field of conservation, this is the key quality of a monument: Free of any rational or scientific quantification and, hence, requiring no expert knowledge, it focuses on the overall experience of time and decay and, in doing so, recognizes a general human need: for patina, for an echo of one's own frailty in the cultural space. For building conservation, this means confronting a paradox that we discussed at the start of this book: the fact that Alterswert, letting something go, over time, so that it slowly decays before eventually achieving the ruinous status of a historical document, will eventually lead to its loss. We cannot want this. One answer would be: Care for the object; establish a relationship in which traces are not removed and empathize with the object in the right way by enabling it to continue existing while also developing new traces, but do not let these harm it. In this sense, use can be a legitimate guideline to building conservation. Furthermore: What we are discussing here is the original mechanism, the phenomenological correspondence between affect and effect that results from our actions and perceptions, which in this case, effectively, are one. Such a relationship with reality significantly alters our perception, affects it retrospectively, and could even be the foundation stone for an analog culture. In this sense, care anchors the building in people's daily lives and, just like the artisan and their piece of work, establishes a relationship between the use, the materiality, and, finally, the atmosphere of the architecture: This is a piece of work that one appropriates through work and whose main use is enhanced by a specific intimacy, a feeling that is familiar to anyone who has become fond of something, taken it empathetically in their hand, and cared for it. One thinks of the positive self-empowerment that comes from *know-how,* from knowing something and being aware of the things surrounding us when we have an active relationship with them as described above by Matthew B. Crawford. Both the house in Monte and the approach taken by Franz Riepl in his work are aptly described by this concept of care. Because care means not just enlivening and maintaining but also repairing. It is becoming clear that building and living and caring and maintaining and Continued Building and caring, etc., make up the larger sensual-phenomenological unit, the arc, which is a circuit that relates to the concept of "participation" and "isolation" and in which design has found its place in the living environment.

The third project in this book, an urban quarter – which represents our third dimensional level after house and settlement – is related to the second aspect of building conservation: the question of the unity and difference between old and new, the overarching relationship permitted by Continued Building. The emergence of contemporary conservation is accompanied by an awareness of the past that, increasingly dominated by institutions and their scholarly vocabulary, creates a distance between past and present, as exemplified by the – more or less – clearly delineated building styles defined by art historians. In the nineteenth century, building conservation involved the rediscovery of stylistic unity and supposedly authentic immediacy that it presumed to create in the present, while modern building conservation in the early twentieth century focused on both the future that was yet to be designed and, increasingly, the past that could be experienced. From this perspective, it is not surprising that until recently – and despite the *Charter of Venice* (1964), which demanded the preservation of context in the sense of the *harmony* of a building[31] – one had to stylize the fracture when something new was added. In contrast, when Michelangelo continued building a church, or Michelozzo a famous Florentine square designed by Filippo Brunelleschi, and thus completed these works because they were able to read the built model and to take this model further in their own way, this was a self-evident process; Brunelleschi himself had already experimented with and continued using older building techniques (including those of Gothic architecture). In today's professional discussion, our sensitive historical awareness has developed into a form of "inclusion," a tacit indication of the transitions – together with reversible interventions, the retention of the ensemble, and a combination of gentle differentiation with the potential use of similar constructional elements – all in the name of a scholarly approach that wants to be able to recognize the different historical layers in the future. Central to this approach are the *absorption* of the old in the new, the expression of the presence of time through patina, and the experience of diachronic layers as a contemporary whole. In other words: It is about today's needs, about an intact spatial experience that we can feel now. And it is about continuity. A continuity, in which design can, by all means, become an archaeological endeavor, as long as harmony does not have to be forced. But how should we practice Continued Building in possibly the most complex structure, a historic city, in a way that meets today's needs and allows the historical layers of the urban fabric to maintain their unity, a task that rarely seems to succeed?

Urban Presence

As well as being a forward-looking design-based activity that diligently works over generations, urban planning is about a community, whose place of political exchange is the city. Furthermore, a society only emerges from the dense clarity of heterogeneous ideas – which find their common purpose in the shared urban realm. In contrast with other notions of the city, Jan Pieper has pointed out that one specific feature of the European city is the way it understands the urban square as a "spatial platform," whose form seeks "to reflect the structure of society by embodying the widely different nuances of the representative and participatory public realm."[32] In contrast with this, it may appear convoluted and dry when separations, alignments, building lines, the number of floors, building type, facade design, greenery, and even rules governing the use of materials, all defined in word and number, serve as the sober origin of this phenomenon. Such requirements or objective design instruments are nothing other than the equivalents of the spatial sensitivity that is at work in the house as a small city and the city as a large house, or ways of formalizing our experiences that are already embedded in the cultural form of the city. They are attempts to objectify our spatial understanding – whether this is latent or based on our conscious experience of urban elements such as the street, square, courtyard, etc., in which actions, encounters ... and yes, again, uses are inscribed. And even if this often appears forgotten in practice, it does not need to be addressed again here for it has long been the subject of relevant treatises such as Camillo Sitte's *Der Städtebau nach seinen künstlerischen Grundsätzen* from 1889.

Generations later, in his *Scientific Autobiography,* Aldo Rossi is more direct: "Each place is remembered to the extent that it becomes a place of affection, or that we identify with it."[33] Feeling and knowing, presence and memory are strangely interwoven in this somewhat enigmatic statement. If one follows Rossi conceptually, this can only mean that the experience of the now and the memory are siblings. That history is dependent upon current experience and that the city as a cultural achievement is always realized in the here and now and only exists as a continuation of the past and the present. "The project itself became a rediscovered object,"[34] is his conclusion for design in general. Design is a process of "discovering" things in a shared space with a history, not of "churning things out." Above, we called it *hervorbringen* "bringing forth." And the city is now its platform, its place. Max Dudler's work belongs to the same tradition, which recognizes the body of the architecture as the basic bearer of experiences – in the urban space that appears to ascribe value through interaction. He has devoted himself to the resilience of the city made of stone, to its Continued Building; mostly in stone and sometimes in brick or even glass. In conversation, he expresses his basic principle as: "Thinking of the future, we place ourselves in a continuity."[35] This requires the space of the *polis* as a place of exchange, in which we can search for context. And he continues: "Only rarely do we show consideration for what has grown, only rarely does modern building establish relationships between things in the wider sense. Creating a new, coherent urban structure within the segmented fabric of the city is a unique urban planning challenge." Wherever Max Dudler and his office successfully apply Continued Building to complex urban situations, he is naturally subject to very intense economic pressure, and yet he always remains true to himself, "idiosyncratic," and refuses to simply align with any ideology. Whenever he works in exceptional places such as Schloss Heidelberg or Hambacher Schloss, we find architectural "complements" to the existing fabric, which almost mimetically complete the history of the notable older buildings and their natural surroundings. At Schloss Heidelberg, which was the subject of a famous debate about conservation around 1900, the new buildings of coarsely cut local stone collect like sedimentation along the heavy wall that already slices through the embankment. His stone structures at Hambacher Schloss, which welcome and accompany visitors, similarly absorb the historic surrounding materiality in elementary volumes that, in turn, appear not abstract but salvaged from the spreading rock until, arriving at the main building, these topographical "fillers" raise the question: Are these the remains of old buildings or new additions? But is this differentiation not senseless, given the obvious focal qualities of memory and spectacle that are triggered by such memorable places? The architect focuses on space and void and encounters – in other words, on urban planning. "Enable things to happen" is another of Rossi's guiding principles.

When this approach is confronted with the task of renewing a country town in Upper Austria, the results are striking. Gallneukirchen, which lies on the Große Gusen and has a population of less than 7,000, is a typical European town, whose form reminds us of its origins: river, bridge, streets that widen to form the main (and market) square opposite the churchyard. All this can still be clearly seen today. In the twentieth century, however, those responsible for the future of such towns felt no obligation to this built spatial logic.

As a result, no one believed that this could be the setting for a model of urban Continued Building, a true contribution to the debate that shows how it could be done. Far away from Europe's major cities, this achievement is solely down to the bold initiative of a family with a long tradition of doing business in the town. In 1993, Anton Riepl began acquiring properties between the historic center and the decidedly rural riverbank;[36] Haslinger Haus, then Haus Nowotny, and then Haus Bodingbauer, etc. There were a total of nine buildings, some already run-down and demolished and others that had to go when work started. This so-called "Riepl Land" between the Gusen, the main street, and Gaisbacher Straße is three times the size of the main square. This means: over 20 years of forward-looking perseverance, developing concepts, changing them, thinking afresh.

It soon becomes clear that the family firm has no more room to grow in this tight urban location just to the south of the main square and the meat processing plant is relocated in the 1990s. But the desire to use the low-density townscape with its green courtyards between the Riepl's hostelry and the river as a trigger for renewing and, at the same time, rethinking Gallneukirchen remains – after all, this is the home of the popular traditional eating place. But what should happen here? Could the area become a huge park? At a certain point, left alone by real estate companies, and with the tacit support of local politicians, it is decided to appoint a project developer. After all, this is a 6,300-square-meter prominently located site, which is completed by purchasing the building at the head of the bridge in 2016. The potential development scenario, which envisages a mix of uses, becomes the basis of an invited competition with international participants, who are selected in line with the project goal of planning a quarter with an urban character. The objective is to lend a hand in those places where, for many reasons, the natural growth of the town has stopped, while creating something that connects with the existing, without turning the clock back. The main aim of the project is that it aligns with the public interest, that the new quarter is accepted and becomes part of Gallneukirchen rather than, as so often, a modern ghost town. The financial risk is considerable and even some existing buildings have to be removed – but this is also an opportunity to create something very different to the monosyllabic residential quarters on the other bank of the Gusen that dilute the edge of the town. Here, at the gateway to the old town, one will soon be able to take a fast train to Linz and the town will become even more attractive and yet no public or cooperative partner can be persuaded to assume responsibility for the mix of shops, offices, and apartments. This leads to concern – which persists until the end of the project – that it may be difficult to maintain control of the development and, hence, ensure that the quality is right and that everyone will be able to identify with the result. In 2019, the opening party takes place – around five years after the competition, the deed is done, despite many risks and uncertainties, such as the groundwater, which menaces the two-story underground garage.

In the new district, we feel neither that we are living in an office zone where suits are obligatory, nor that the town has lost any dignity nor become a trivialized, purely private place. There is a clear differentiation between street, square, and courtyard and we do not even see the inevitable chain stores lining the pavements. Parked underground, the cars have disappeared from this part of town. One drives into the garage at the head of the bridge, drives out

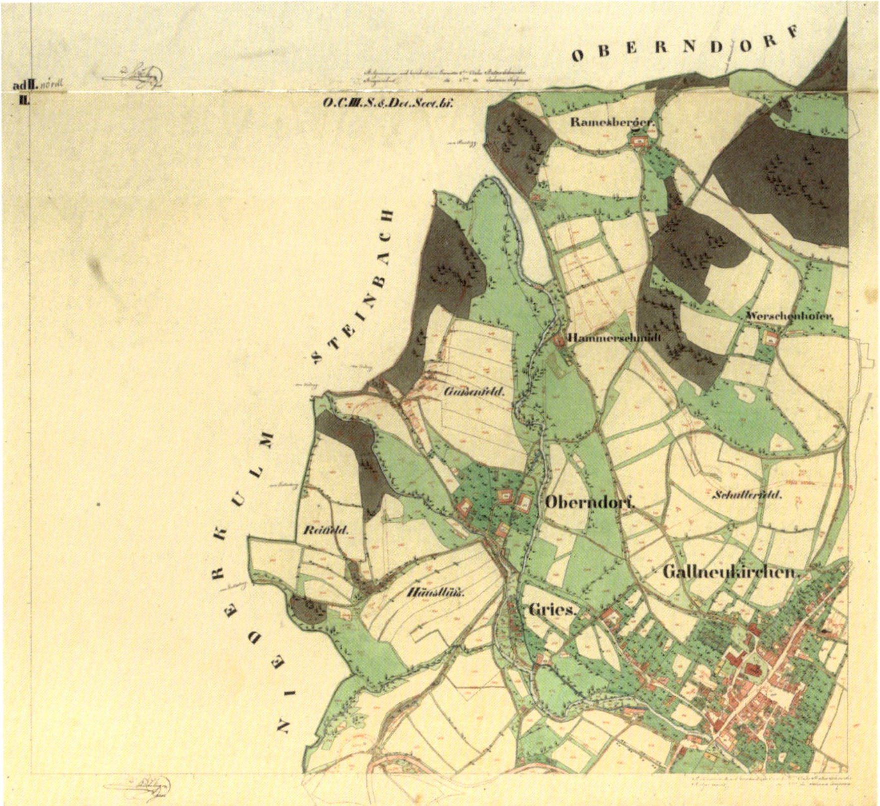
OBERNDORF
O.C.III.S.&.Dec.Sect.bf.
Ramesberger.
STEINBACH
NIEDERKULM
Hammerschmidt
Werschenhofer.
Gaisenfeld.
Oberndorf.
Schullerfeld.
Reitfeld.
Gallneukirchen.
Häusllüs.
Gries.

GALLNEUKIRCHEN O.Ö. FLIEGERAUFNAHME NR. 2

at the other end of the district and lives an urban life, while enjoying the views of the surrounding hills. One shops as if one is in a shopping center, but one is not. And, above all, the new built fabric plugs into the old town, but equally presents itself as a new district. The "supermarket problem" – the constant desire of the public to be able to choose from lots of products at once – has also been solved, for this is hidden in the heart of the ensemble, albeit not underground. Thanks to the height of the space, which is a sort of gallery, the light comes from outside and above. The entrance to the gallery doubles as the main portal to the new quarter, which is also right next to the historic head of the bridge; two open stone stairs convey pedestrians to the new open spaces. Incidentally, this is another reason why this is a piece of city, because rights of way have been preserved and the apartments have many different owners. Thirty apartments with between 54 and 135 square meters are laid out to meet a wide range of needs; they have a total area of 2,500 square meters, with 3,800 being occupied by shops and restaurants and around 3,000 by office space.

The solution that led to Max Dudler's success against the impressive list of competitors – the result of his expert, urban planner's interpretation of the plot ratios and spatial program – consists of density and mix, a combination of a range of activities in one building, and an approach in which the volumes are only ostensibly an erratic fabric of stand-alone structures based on a system of urban building lines, boundaries, and routes, etc. For this fabric is derived from the existing and it is this that lends it its form, which is then refined, physically and spatially improved – addressed as a network of in-between spaces – in a series of revision phases. As a result, the new

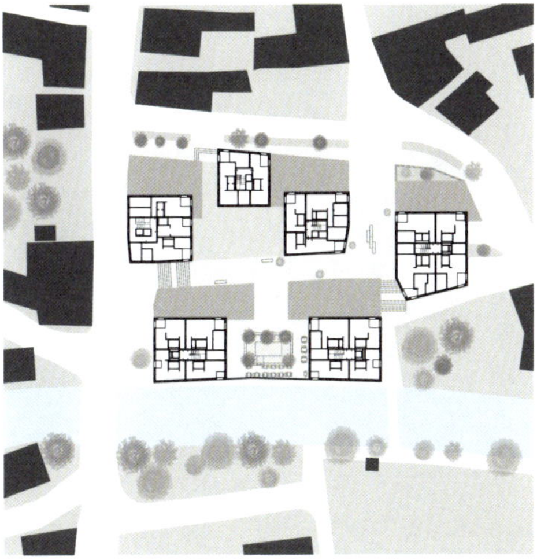

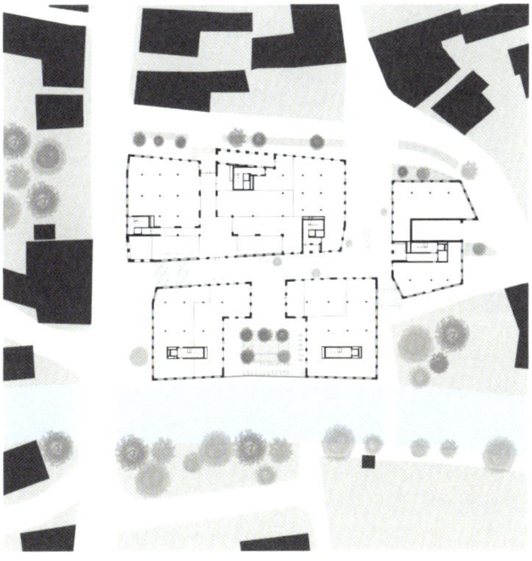

Urban quarter "One", Gallneukirchen, residential level; commercial zone
Architect Max Dudler

One
Am Sonntag
ÖSTERREICH
lesen!

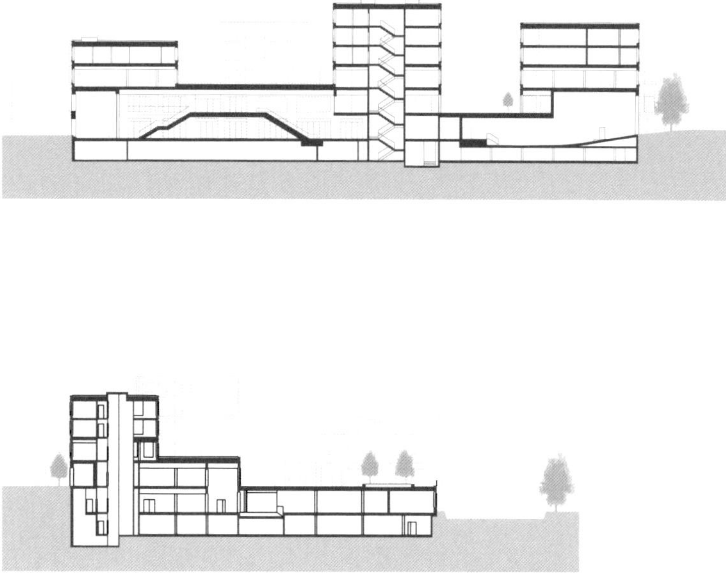

Urban quarter "One", Gallneukirchen, longitudinal and transverse sections
Architect Max Dudler

quarter is informed by situatedness, looking, moving, and resting, in both the public and private realms. The streetfront facades are stepped in height. Above the commercial zone we find the offices, partly set back, behind which the residential towers grow skywards, with loggias in every unit and floor plans that turn the corner. In this way, new streets and two new squares emerge from an imaginary form that is defined by interpolating the texture and topography of the existing. Furthermore, we can speak of a model for other towns and cities because local factors were also decisive in this project: The new district may be higher and bulkier and might initially seem to breach the scale of historic Gallneukirchen, but it confidently starts with the most recent, structured expansion of the town at the end of the nineteenth century, which is reactivated by Max Dudler's concept: On the opposite side of the main street we find the evangelical vicarage in the Biedermeier style and the massive Haus Bethanien, the mother house of the deaconesses from 1909, while the project's eastern neighbor is Haus Zoar, another building of several stories that was built in 1884. The new district completes this ring of exemplary structures and absorbs their impulse: in terms of height and grain, but also in the reinterpretation of their facades, with which it addresses the main street. The appearance and character of the buildings were issues for a long time. But the stone facades slowly evolved into a series of layers created from primary stone frames and a range of plaster surfaces that transform them into visually enchanting reliefs. Hence, the design is not the result of abstract dimensional rules or rigid tectonics and the existing exercises its influence in a, partly, new way through the visual references to the classical order of the neighboring buildings – for those, who want to see this. The final impression is one of elegance and haptic. This enhances daily life in the small town without overwhelming it, is both reserved and urban. To be "urban" – to be refined and to refine – is the general aspiration of this architecture, an aspiration that it communicates to all who pause to address it.

Developing the Senses

Those who have read this far, who have immersed themselves in this investigation of theory and built form and held the course, should have heard a plea that concerns us all: Because it is based on our shared experience, our (constantly) critical perception, which we perhaps do not interrogate, nourish, sharpen, or challenge enough – or, having doing so, employ against the dominating *logic* that has long since taken hold of our living environment. The book should encourage, in broad terms, the adoption of a specific perspective that has been described as phenomenological. It has sought to bring together some not so well-known examples of current practice with theory. The book has few footnotes and no exhausting explanations of the terminology, in order to remain understandable, even though it follows academic conventions. This special perspective – which the book adopts with the help of the selected model buildings – is its actual message.

Is it not the case that all the arts recognize the existing as their starting point? We learn at school about the artists who set out to experience the real world as a means of renewing and advancing their discipline. It goes without saying that we educate ourselves on the basis of existing things, for how does one evolve if not through dialog? We can only be stimulated by a concrete counterpart, by the phenomena that we are involved in every day, that instigate, enrich, and remain present in the cycle of experience, activity, experience. And even when experience is a mere memory or is contained within a work, when it is, in a certain sense, "recounted" to us and we appear to be passive – when reading a book or hearing music, in the space of a book or of a concert, etc. –, when we, in other words, empathize with the things around us, even then the power of our human imagination is based on the sensual-material experiences that we are able to transmit and emphatically reanimate. Just like the heavy stone on a pillar or the tensile strength of a brick arch, in order to experience something we first require the weight of our own body as a reference. Concreteness and idea, reality and design are directly connected. This is the essence of the architectural: Creating space from concrete experience, shaped by the existing, integrated in the intentionality of our relationships. Architecture is concrete; that space, which we not only use but in which we experience spatiality. The content of the space that we create and experience is physical; material, context, and form are inseparably intertwined in this space with our senses and, thus, it is also an idea and part of the cultural history of things. A condition can be applied to this analog relationship: We must have experienced something. We must have lived in and with this world.

Perhaps this appears too insignificant – this appreciation of the concrete in a digital age. But the thoughts in this book are based on this simple but momentous idea that concreteness is the essence and starting point of the architectural. Our bodies need shelter, but it is only through the cognitive recognition of the satisfaction obtained from the sensual experience that we can develop ideas about how to build this shelter in a reasonable way.

If this plea concludes with this shortened and oversimplified recapitulation and, in essence, repeatedly refers to three buildings from the recent history of architecture as highly varied counter models to the current built reality, this is not simply because it can seem so difficult to become positively engaged with our surroundings on a sensual level. Such a lament would be too trite and immediately attract objections. Three buildings with three different urban scales – a house, a settlement, and an urban quarter – and different origins and approaches provide the framework of the narrative: that the continuity of well-built space has given way to isolated sensations, and that we no longer seek satisfaction in shared private or communal space. But *satisfaction* cannot come from sensations that wrench us from our everyday lives. And our everyday lives are not gray: Where and how do we situate ourselves on a daily basis, how do we meet the many challenges in our living environment, win the battle for survival in our competitive society? Architecture cannot avoid these questions and should not aim to become a system of architectural approaches that are largely incompatible, for is it not our current task to shape everyday life in such a way that it is more sustainable? And the model for addressing this task – if it did not already exist, we would be right to create it – is it not to be found in the inherent possibilities of the concrete world? Once again, poetry means: *to bring forth* – out of the wealth of the existing, a wealth that first becomes visible in poetic dialog. It concerns the atmosphere of things and, hence, the materiality, spatiality, construction, and contextuality of the existing. The beauty of this is the symmetry of perception and doing, which involves all of us – not just a single profession.

Astonishingly, during the decades of modernist progress, the built world has experienced constant quantitative and technical growth, in terms of the area of living space or the consumption of resources or land – and yet the contrast with the past is intriguing: Compared with the experiential wealth offered by the world around us, which is not a machine for spectacle and consumption, the balance is hugely negative. This is why it is important to question the increased degree of freedom of the individual. Which freedom? This and GDP are the benchmarks of today's society. But this approach ignores so much. The loss of historical diversity in our urban spaces is enough to underline this: Facades, shops, and streets are commercial and leave no trace. Buildings have a half-life similar to that of clothes. The only occasional exceptions can be found in the city centers that are treated like museum objects, but these appear strangely alien, out of sorts, and mutate into hollowed-out advertising hoardings for the past. Overshadowed only by a general concern for the future that can arise during times of crisis, the thing that most troubles us today (with good reason) is agrarian monocultures. But can technology solve our problems? Or do we need a new approach – not to technology but to our whole way of living? Can we still imagine a life other than a consumerist one? And what can architecture do to facilitate this? A simple thought: the fact that we are less and less able to stay in one place. Perhaps this is the reason for and the scourge of our crisis: a loss of places that are rich with experience; experience, with which they satisfy us and that allows us to identify with them and want to shape them by staying put. And it could also be that the experiences offered by staying in such places are simply no longer enough.

The selection of the three projects discussed above was delicate, because they have to be projects that represent something, without taking themselves too seriously. They have to be both exemplary and comprehensible. They are also the model for the ideas of a new architectural phenomenology and its central concepts of tolerance, concreteness, atmosphere, and unavailability. This is where we find the challenge of our time, to make things happen starting from this built center, from this architecture of the everyday. And yet, the special is disappearing towards the very edge of this world – no real experience without a long-distance flight and no nature outside nature reserves, etc. What else can this center be, other than the shared reality in which we all participate, including architects, who also only begin as participants? But when our design work only focuses on our abstract, professionalized activity it seems clear that we cannot be paying enough attention to this supposed ordinariness. This is why we need a phenomenological perspective. For design, this is something that emerges from everyday life, that is no different from being in the midst of things, but that still offers the opportunity to comment on the basis of and about this experience and, therefore, about change. After all, this is architecture's potential space: the contemplation of what could be. And this is where we find a future that can be created from the existing.

Continued Building is the dialogical design principle that underlies this. This is not a dialog with one's own creativity, or with the possibilities of the brief, the potential of a program, the cost parameters, and not even with the clients. To some extent it is about institutional building conservation, upcycling, the culture of conversion, etc. But, more than everything else, this book is a plea for presence, for our experience of the present, as a starting point for being "wide awake" when we design. For then, designing would be nothing other than a certain way of living.

The Concreteness of Things

1 Stephen Bates, Jonathan Sergison, "Resistance," *2G, Sergison Bates,* no. 34 (2005), 133.

2 Ibid.

3 Ibid, 131f.

4 Christian Norberg-Schulz, *Genius loci. Landschaft, Lebensraum, Baukunst* (Stuttgart: Klett-Cotta, 1982), 8f.

5 Stephen Bates, Jonathan Sergison, "Working with Tolerance," in *arq Architectural Research Quarterly,* no. 3/3, (1999), 221.

6 Hartmut Rosa, *Resonance. A Sociology of Our Relationship to the World,* trans. James C. Wagner (New Jersey: Wiley, 2019).

7 Bates, Sergison, "Working with Tolerance," 223.

8 Kenneth Frampton, "Ten Points on an Architecture of Regionalism. A Provisional Polemic," in *Center,* no. 3 (1987), 27.

9 Bates, Sergison, "Working with Tolerance," 231.

10 Cf. Soetsu Yanagi, "The Beauty of Miscellaneous Things" (1926), in *The Beauty of Everyday Things* (London: Penguin, 2018), 26–57.

11 Matthew B. Crawford, *The World Beyond Your Head: On Becoming an Individual in an Age of Distraction* (New York: Farrar, 2016), 23, 27.

12 Scott Wheland Wall and Juhani Pallasmaa, "Common Ground: An Interview with Juhani Pallasmaa," in *Journal of Architectural Education,* vol. 63, no. 1 (2009), 77.

13 Juhani Pallasmaa, *Six themes for the next millennium* (1994), www.thefreelibrary.com/Six+themes+for+the+next+millenium.-a015718505

14 Christian Norberg-Schulz, *Man's Home,* https://arkitektur-n.no/artikler/menneskenes-bolig-ncs

The Atmosphere of the Ordinary

15 Albert Kirchengast, Hans Kolb (eds.), *Franz Riepl Über Architektur* (Salzburg: Müry Salzmann, 2015), 15. Some of the quotes in this book come from conversations with Franz Riepl in 2022.

16 Albert Kirchengast, Hans Kolb (eds.), "Über das ‚Griffige'. Im Gespräch mit Franz Riepl," in *Franz Riepl baut auf dem Land. Eine Ästhetik des Selbstverständlichen* (Basel: Birkhäuser, 2018), 99, trans. R. H.

17 Adolf Loos, "Rules for Those Building in the Mountains" (1913), in *Ornament and Crime,* trans. Shaun Whiteside (London: Penguin, 2019), 213-18.

18 Adolf Loos, "Architektur" (1910), in *The Architecture of Adolf Loos,* trans. Wilfried Wang (London: Arts Council, 1985), 108.

19 Peter Zumthor, *Atmospheres. Architectural Environments. Surrounding Objects* (Basel: Birkhäuser, 2006), 19.

20 Ibid., 15.

21 Emanuele Coccia, *Sinnenleben. Eine Philosophie* (Munich: Carl Hanser, 2020), 9, trans. R. H.

22 Dagobert Frey, "Wesensbestimmung der Architektur" (Lecture 1923), in *Zeitschrift für Ästhetik und Allgemeine Kunstwissenschaft* (1925), 73, trans. R. H.

23 Adolf Loos, "On Thrift" (1924), in *Ornament and Crime*, 245-66,

24 Adalbert Stifter, *Motley Stones* (1853), trans. Isabel Fargo Cole (New York: NYRB, 2021), 3-8.

The Presence of History

25 Martin Boesch, "Das Neue im Alten. Zum architektonischen Umgang mit Bestehendem," in *werk, bauen + wohnen. Nahtstellen*, vol. 1/2 (2019), 15.

26 Hans-Georg Gadamer, *The Relevance of the Beautiful*, trans. Nicholas Walker (Cambridge: CUP, 1977), 49, with thanks to Thomas Will for the tip.

27 Arne Naess, "Self-realization: An Ecological Approach to Being in the World" (1986), in Alan Drengson & Yuichi Inoue (eds.), *The Deep Ecology Movement, An Introductory Anthology* (Berkeley: North Atlantic Books, 1995), 29.

28 Henry David Thoreau, *Walden or, Life in the Woods* (1854), (Boston: Houghton Mifflin, 1893), 153.

29 Cf: Alois Riegl, "Die Stimmung als Inhalt der modernen Kunst" (1889), in Riegl, *Gesammelte Aufsätze* (Vienna: WUV, 1996), 27–37.

30 Alois Riegl, *Der moderne Denkmalkultus. Sein Wesen und seine Entstehung* (Vienna: Braumüller, 1903).

31 "Replacements of missing parts must integrate harmoniously with the whole, but at the same time must be distinguishable from the original so that restoration does not falsify the artistic or historic evidence". (*Charter of Venice*, 1964, Article 12).

32 Jan Pieper, "Der Platz – ein Grundelement der europäischen Stadt," in Christoph Mäckler (ed.), *Handbuch der Stadtbaukunst, Band 3 – Platzräume* (Dortmund: Deutsches Institut für Stadtbaukunst, 2022), 8, trans. R. H.

33 Aldo Rossi, *A Scientific Autobiography*, trans. Lawrence Venuti (Boston: MIT, 1981), 41.

34 Ibid., 11.

35 Max Dudler, "Rebuilding the City or: Keeping the Ball Close," in J. Christoph Bürkle (ed.), *Max Dudler. Architecture for the City* (Salenstein: Niggli, 2003), 116.

36 Anton Riepl is the nephew of Franz Riepl, whose support for this undertaking was decisive.

Photo Credits

9 Historical brick wall, England; Photo: Stephen Bates, London

19 Val di Muggio, Ticino, spring 2022; Photo: Albert Kirchengast, Vienna

21–24, 31–34, 41 House in Monte, Ticino, Renovation Jonathan Sergison; Photo: Hélène Binet, London

27 House in Cadaqués, staircase, Spain, Renovation Stephen Bates; Photo: Hélène Binet, London

45 Dambachmayrhof, barn, Kematen, Architect Franz Riepl; Photo: Alex Krischner, Graz; with thanks to Alex Krischner

53 Bindermichl, panoramic view looking east, Linz, 2.9.1954; Source: Nordico Stadtmuseum, Linz, NA-027332; Aerial photography Hans Wöhrl

54 Wohnhof Bindermichl, Linz, April 1947; Source: Archives of the City of Linz

61–65, 67–68, 72, 80 Bindermichl, Linz, Renovation Franz Riepl; Photo: David Schreyer, Wörgl

94 Hambacher Schloss, Restoration Max Dudler; Photo: Stefan Müller, Berlin

99 Historical cadaster, original map 2, Gallneukirchen, 1826; Source: Federal Office of Metrology and Surveying, Vienna; with thanks to Franz Riepl

100 Postcard of Gallneukirchen, 1950s; Source: Fotoklub Gallneukirchen; with thanks to Erwin Doppler

101 Urban quarter "One", aerial view, Gallneukirchen; Source: Private archive Anton Riepl, Gallneukirchen

104–105, 109, 111 Urban quarter "One", Gallneukirchen, Architect Max Dudler; Photo: David Schreyer, Wörgl

106–108, 110, 115–116 Urban quarter "One", Gallneukirchen, Architect Max Dudler; Photo: Stefan Müller, Berlin

Biographies

Max Dudler is an architect and town planner with offices in Berlin, Frankfurt/Main, Munich, and Zurich. He has been a professor at the Kunstakademie Düsseldorf since 2004.

Franz Riepl has been a self-employed architect since 1967 and was Professor of Agricultural Building and Rural Settlement at Graz University of Technology between 1980 and 2000.

Jonathan Sergison is a co-founder of Sergison Bates architects, which is based in London and Zurich. He has been a professor at the Academy of Architecture in Mendrisio since 2008.

Albert Kirchengast has been Junior Professor for Architectural Theory at BTU Cottbus-Senftenberg since 2022 and is an author of publications on the history and theory of modernism.

Acknowledgments

to Franz Riepl and Hans Kolb; the architects Max Dudler and Jonathan Sergison; to David Marold and Bettina R. Algieri of Birkhäuser Verlag; to Juan Carlos Gómez and Florian Schuchlenz for adapting the plans; to all archives and to the photographers, who captured the buildings that we must still encounter for ourselves.

Author
Albert Kirchengast, A-Vienna

Acquisitions Editor
David Marold, Birkhäuser Verlag, A-Vienna

Content & Production Editor
Bettina R. Algieri, Birkhäuser Verlag, A-Vienna

Translation German/English
Rupert Hebblethwaite, A-Vienna

Layout, cover design, typography
Albert Kirchengast, A-Vienna

Adaptation of plans
Juan Carlos Gómez and Florian Schuchlenz, A-Graz

Image editing
Pixelstorm, A-Vienna

Printing
Holzhausen, the book-printing brand of Gerin Druck GmbH

This book is the fourth volume in the series *Baukulturaria* from the Verein zur Erhaltung und Erforschung der österreichischen Baukultur.

Series Editors
Hans Kolb, A-Graz, and Albert Kirchengast, A-Vienna

Library of Congress Control Number: 2022948606

Bibliographic information published by the German National Library
The German National Library lists this publication in the Deutsche Nationalbibliografie; detailed bibliographic data are available on the Internet at http://dnb.dnb.de.

ISBN 978-3-0356-2650-6
e-ISBN (PDF) 978-3-0356-2651-3

German Print ISBN 978-3-0356-2649-0

P.O. Box 44, 4009 Basel, Switzerland

Part of Walter de Gruyter GmbH, Berlin/Boston

9 8 7 6 5 4 3 2 1 www.birkhauser.com